The Limelight

The Limelight
A Compendium of Contemporary Columbia Artists
Volume II

Edited by Cynthia Boiter

Muddy Ford Press

Chapin, South Carolina

THE LIMELIGHT: A COMPENDIUM OF CONTEMPORARY COLUMBIA ARTISTS, VOLUME II. Copyright 2015 by Cynthia Boiter. All rights reserved. Printed in the United States of America. No part of this book may be used or reproduced in any manner whatsoever without written permission except in the case of brief quotations embodied in critical articles and reviews. For information address Muddy Ford Press, 1009 Muddy Ford Road, Chapin, South Carolina 29036.

Library of Congress Number: 2013931882

ISBN: 978-1-942081-03-6

Cover Art by Matt Catoe

Terry—played by Claire Bloom: "I thought you hated the theatre?"

Calvero—played by Charlie Chaplin: "I also hate the sight of blood, but it's in my veins."

From the film The Limelight, 1952

Created when an oxyhydrogen flame is directed at a cylinder of calcium oxide, known as quicklime, the limelight was first used in London's Covent Garden Theatre in 1837 to illuminate the stars of the stage.

CONTENTS

Preface   1
By Cynthia Boiter

Nostalgia, Memories, and Records: Iron & Wine's Sam Beam   5
By Kyle Petersen

The Art of Healing: Jeanee Bourque   13
By Jane Gari

Turning "Shit" into Art: Gina Langston Brewer   19
By Kristine Hartvigsen

An Ethereal Talent: Lynn Burgess   25
By Laurie Brownell McIntosh

My Rainbow Chasing Muse: Robert Clark   29
By Tom Poland

And Then She Gave Me a Song: Deborah Deck   37
By Debra Daniel

A Vital Force: Cynthia Gilliam   43
By August Krickel

A Gentle Southern Voice: Bentz Kirby   53
By James D. McCallister

Where the Poet Dwells & the Private Religion of Grief: Ed Madden   63
By Jennifer Bartell

How to Bake the Perfect Loaf of Bread: Marion Mason   69
By Kara M Gunter

Superhero: Darion McCloud   77
By Jon Tuttle

Remembering: Carrie McCray   85
By Randy Spencer

A Love Letter: Ray McManus   93
By Susan Levi Wallach

The Drama of Writing: Cassie Premo Steele   101
By Brandi L. Perry

My Nemesis and Me: Susan Lenz on Wim Roefs   109
By Susan Lenz

The Art and the Artist: Boyd Saunders   127
By Rachel Haynie

More Than a Story: Homer "Pappy" Sherrill   137
By Michael Miller

There's Still Some Room at the Table: George Singleton   145
By William Garland

A Man, a Tam, and a Guitar: Drink Small, the Blues Doctor   149
By Clair DeLune

Driving Toward the Desert: Paul Kaufman   155
By Chad Henderson

About the Authors   165

About the Cover Art   171

Preface

By Cynthia Boiter

No one who knows anything about the life of an artist—visual, performing, or written word—would ever call it easy. Between finding funding, finding time, and finally convincing your family that, yes, one can legitimately claim "artist" as an occupation, sometimes all that is left is the calling to create. What would be easy, however, would be to re-paint the struggles of living the life of an artist in a manner in which the individual artist claims no responsibility for these difficulties, or worse, blames their fellow artists. You've heard it all before—the fight for funding, the rumors of favoritism in the media, the crediting connections, family, or friends for another artist's success. It can be all too convenient.

Happily and by some miracle of shining light and stardust, the Columbia, South Carolina arts community has, for the most part, escaped these pitfalls of ease and convenience that can be so detrimental to a community. This collection of essays is a testament to that fact. Columbia artists have cultivated a reputation for warm comradery both within and between arts disciplines. Barely a month goes by in which one or another group of writers, painters, or musicians doesn't gather together to launch a new project, unveil a new collaboration, or raise funds for a fellow artist in need. Recently, during early discussions about a new visual arts award, more than one artist registered their concerns about competing against their colleagues whose friendship they so cherished.

The hard truth is that Columbia artists recognize that we live in a larger local culture that can be, at best, ambivalent about the arts, and at times, downright discouraging. Rather than enjoying the favors of a state government that values the arts and rewards us with grants or subsidies, we have to fight for the financial pittance we're allocated.

But we fight together.

Columbia artists know the value of the inspiration that comes from watching an artist from a discipline different from one's own perform, exhibit, or read. The investment in having the back of the sculptor in the studio next door. The all-encompassing importance of a healthy and functional community and the privileges that community provides. In her essay on printmaker Boyd Saunders, for example, writer Rachel Haynie talks about the longevity of Boyd's relationships. "If ever you were in the fold of Boyd Saunders, you remain in that fold," she writes. "That, about Boyd, inspires and motivates me, and it affects so many others in similar ways."

Writer Tom Poland, shares a similar value for relationships and talks with affection about his long-time collaborative partner, photographer Robert Clark, and his ability to glean almost-magical beauty from nature in its normal state. Tom calls it, "the Vision of Glittering Potential, an intuition for splendor," and discusses at length the many lessons he has learned from his friend.

Lessons learned are a common thread throughout this collection. Visual artist Kara Gunter and writer Debra Daniel both talk about the early influences of teachers and how the seeds they planted have bloomed into the careers both women enjoy today. In poet Jennifer Bartell's essay on her mentor, Ed Madden, she acknowledges not the skills of wordsmithing he taught her, but rather how, in dealing with his father's death, Ed helped her learn how to deal with the passing of her own father. "As poets we reach out into the darkness attempting to solve the riddle of the great weight of death and grief," she writes. "… Ed has taught me how to navigate the reef of grief. And that is the lesson I will always treasure most."

Some folks write about their friends, and the love and admiration for their work and talent shines through as something pure and pristine. About musician-lawyer Bentz Kirby, Don McCallister writes, "His musical energy seemed boundless." Playwright Jon Tuttle calls multi-talented theatre artist Darion McCloud nothing short of a superhero. But it's not always a Stepford Valley friend fest. In visual artist Susan Lenz's departure from the typical accolade-filled piece, she calls gallery owner Wim Roefs, the subject of her essay, her nemesis, declaring his reticence to accept her work as real art to be the personal challenge she needed to persevere against a number of odds, including her own self-doubt. Susan, whose work in fiber art and installation is internationally known and admired, concludes her essay with a loving message to the man who, to her, is the master of her exile, proving once again that love can be both capricious and transformative.

Enjoy these essays of love, admiration, challenge, and inspiration and, in so doing, make yourself at home in the warm and welcoming community of Columbia, SC artists and authors. It's no easier being an artist here than it is anywhere else but, as this collection of essays clearly attests, it is endlessly more rewarding.

July 2015

Nostalgia, Memories, and Records: Iron & Wine's Sam Beam

By Kyle Petersen

Every music fan has loads of records that they can tell you their own personal stories about. Sometimes these stories are fascinating and illuminating in their ability to stumble on some precious truth about the nature of music or capture a particular moment in time that manages to tell us something about an entire generation or American culture as a whole. Most, I would reckon, fall somewhere uneasily in between the two.

I don't really know where on that continuum my story about Sam Beam's songs lays. But here it is anyway.

———

When I was in high school, I desperately wanted the music I loved to tell you something about me. Which, looking back on it, it probably did, just not in the way I intended it to at the time. Those four years saw my tastes shift every few months, adding and subtracting new bands and old as I gradually (and painfully) disengaged from rock and Top 40 radio, dug through my dad's record collection, and entrusted my fortunes to the very hit-and-miss review section of *Rolling Stone* magazine. As a freshman I was entangled in the grips of post-grunge and nu-metal; by senior year, I was riding a new wave of indie rock bands in the mainstream and a burgeoning, almost all-consuming interest in alt-country.

The university and my stint doing college radio at WUSC invariably shifted my understanding and relationship to music after that, for better and worse, but I still look back at those uncertain and tentative days to try to understand why I ended up caring about music so much and trying to write about it as best I can.

That Sam Beam's records, under the Iron & Wine moniker, came out during this period is of course mostly coincidental, but I can't help but think of how much they defined me as a listener. For one, Beam's story is the kind of fodder a budding music obsessive can obsess over. His debut album, *The Creek Drank the Cradle*, was essentially a collection of demos that managed to make it into the hands of Jonathan Poneman, cofounder of Sub Pop Records, one of the biggest independent labels in the world. Before the label signed Beam, he was making a living as a film professor in Florida while recording these quiet, hushed folk songs at night and overdubbing various stringed instrument parts himself. I'm not sure if Beam ever actually said this, but part of the mythos of the album was that he sang and played so quietly in an effort not to wake up his three young girls at the time. Can you beat that?

―――

It wasn't until later that I would connect the other dots in this story—that Beam had grown up in Chapin, South Carolina, and was good friends with Michael Bridwell, the brother of Band of Horses leader Ben Bridwell, whose family lived in Irmo. These Midlands connections, oddly enough, are what led Beam on the path to a fecund music career that hasn't slowed down since.

That part doesn't matter so much to my personal story, about what those early Iron & Wine records meant to me.

While *Creek* was the only Beam-only release aside from a couple of EPs, His fairly restrained follow-up *Our Endlessly Numbered Days* came out my senior year, as well as the career-shifting *Woman King* EP, which signaled a move towards full band arrangements and stylistic experimentation. These three recordings, along with some soundtrack cuts like his take on the Postal Service's "Such Great Heights" and his epic ballad "The Trapeze Swinger," were the canon that I worshiped under.

Looking back on it now, part of the appeal was surely somewhat conceptual. Beam was and is an impressive lyric writer, and his tendency towards elliptical metaphors and haunting one-liners is like kryptonite for a music fan trying to escape the horrifying sense that their interest in popular music is facile. There's also his engagement with explicitly Southern imagery, something my suburban high school self yearned for in ways that I still don't really understand. The tangle of guitars and other stringed instruments he overdubbed on top of these songs often felt an obscuring web, giving a sense of complexity that was also probably comforting.

In the broad tapestry of the popular music tradition, Beam belongs to a distinct sub-group of singer/songwriters who writer serious, dense songs that halfway aspire to poetry while, at the same, crafting distinct melodies and vocal personas that make their work often appear inscrutable on paper. People like Bob Dylan or Nick Drake are his most obvious forbearers, although there are touches of the button-down pop cleverness of Paul Simon and the single-minded irascibility of Neil Young as well.

That the comparisons I'm making here are no coincidence—Beam, while arguably one of the primary figures in the rise of the bearded indie rock folkie phenomenon, has remained remarkably aloft and removed from easy pigeonholing within contemporary music, especially with his later recordings, which are largely premised on using his songs as broad sonic canvasses full of horns, junkyard percussion, and unorthodox arrangements.

Most of the appeal even now, though, comes from the emotional connections and possibility of what Beam alone does with his voice, words, and melodies. And while I appreciate and even love some of those latter-day albums, I can't, on a primal level, shake that early stuff.

———

I still remember the first time I got to listen to *Creek*. I had just purchased it from the soon-to-be-closed Millennium Music in Charleston, and I popped it in to my portable CD player while on a crowded bus of fellow high school seniors. Listening to that record with headphones, particularly in a noisy, claustrophobic space, is to be transported somewhere else entirely. Beam's warm melodies and hushed voice are like someone whispering in your ear, creating a space for contemplation and small pleasures in a world that seemingly will have none of it.

———

I also have a very specific memory of riding around Lowcountry back roads with the scenery full of kudzu listening to *Days* and feeling like, for once, I had found an album that made sense for where I lived. At the time I don't think I even knew he was from South Carolina.

———

My high school girlfriend was a huge *Garden State* fan, particularly the soundtrack, and I liked it quite a bit, too. But I don't have much in the way of distinct memories connecting her to Iron & Wine's contribution to the soundtrack, "Such Great Heights," nor does that movie strongly resonate with why I love Iron & Wine.

Instead, it the extensive use of his songs in the less-successful film from the following year, *In Good Company*, that sticks with me. For all its flaws, it's a subtler and more emotionally complicated film than *Garden State*, and it's very direct engagement with family, life choices, and the complex interiority of individuals works better for Beam's songs.

But really, it's not the usage of the music in the film itself that sticks in my gut. What actually sticks with me is cruising around with that girlfriend listening to that soundtrack (David Byrne, Aretha Franklin, Peter Gabriel, and Steely Dan alongside The Shins and Iron & Wine) and hearing "Trapeze Swinger" for the first time. It was near the end of our relationship, and that whole song, with its insistent refrain to "remember me" and its nostalgic evocations of childhood and first romance mixed with concerns about mortality and the afterlife, hit like a ton of bricks.

―――

Going to Bonnaroo Music Festival in 2005, after I had graduated college and broken up with that girlfriend, was a really big deal for me. I had wanted to go the year before, but it actually felt more right this time around, on the precipice of a new chapter in my life while teetering precariously on the last one.

And I probably saw something like twenty bands that weekend—among them The Mars Volta, The Allman Brothers Band, John Prine, My Morning Jacket, Rilo Kiley, and Modest Mouse—but it was special, above all, because I got to see Iron & Wine perform for the first time.

It was raining for most of that set, something that felt oddly appropriate given the cozy nature of the songs and the safety that his tent show provided the adoring audience. Even when the far-off echoes of The Black Crowes' wailing Southern boogie rock intruded on the moment, it felt right, almost as if we had found a shelter of intimacy amidst the aural carnage of a giant music festival like Bonnaroo.

At this point Beam was bound and determined to move to full-band status, and even delivered a rollicking take on Buffalo Springfield's "Mr. Soul" that made ample use of his two percussionists. Still, it was when he sent everyone away save for his sister Sarah to sing harmonies that haunted me, calling up the ghosts of so many memories and private moments spent just listening to his songs.

He encored with "The Trapeze Swinger." At this point, I hadn't been to many concerts before, especially not many given by the musicians who were now dominating my headspace. It felt like the world moved.

—

Fast forward almost a decade later to this past winter, where Beam was doing a rare solo tour without his usual Iron & Wine band mates. He was coming through Charleston in February, so I took the opportunity to grab an in-person interview where I attempted to connect the dots between his experience growing up in Chapin and my coming of age in the Lowcountry.

He was amiable to answer my questions, even thoughtful, but I got the sense that he wasn't too tied to the idea that his sense of place as a child and the musician and writer he would become were that connected, beyond the fact that it was occasional subject matter for him. He talked a bit about visiting his grandparents on their farm in Chester and a few other experiences of rural Southern traditionalism, but mostly he talked about listening to the radio, his parents' record collections, and discovering "other" cool music, like Joy Division, that wasn't on the radio through friends and record stores—he even name-checks Manifest.

Leaving the interview it felt like one of those times when I, the ever-awkward and over-eager music writer, tried too hard to force ideas, connections, and words that were never meant to be, but now I think I was wrong. I think Beam was, unintentionally, kind of telling the same story as mine—that of a kid from the South growing up with nebulous conceptions of region and place but a decisive sense, if not firm understanding, of the fact that they loved, and cared about music. That it did something for him as a kid, and that kind of emotional relationship carried over to the music he would make all those years later.

Even if that's not what he was getting at and I missed the point again, it sure is nice to think so.

―――

After the interview I hang around the Charleston Music Hall to catch the show. It had been many years since I'd actually gotten a chance to see Beam play, and he'd put out a couple of excellent LPs since then, so I wasn't expecting a set list of all my old favorites or anything. And sure enough, he pulled fairly evenly from across his career with the casual and assured effortlessness of the truly great songwriter that he is. I was put in touch, all over again, with the magic that drew me to his work in the first place.

If I had to do it all over again, I probably wouldn't have done the interview. I didn't need the journalistic digging, the concrete details or conceptually flimsy conjectures.

All I really needed was the music and the memories, intertwining together, one more time.

The Art of Healing: Jeanee Bourque

By Jane Gari

Mammograms are awkward. I'd been warned by other women about the uncomfortable squishing that comes from having your breast turned into a pancake between two slabs of glass. I was prepared for physical discomfort. That's something you can brace yourself for. But the psychological underpinnings of diagnostic examinations have always unnerved me.

My personal reaction to fear in the context of a doctor's office or hospital is to talk a lot and try to be funny. The rationale for this is something like, "If I'm dying or gravely ill they'll stop me from being so glib and corny and cut to the chase. But if everyone continues to laugh and keep it light, I'm okay. Everything's okay." I apply this logic to every real and potential medical crisis I face, and my first mammogram was no different. The technician who put my breasts in a vice and told me that, "breasts are like snowflakes" seemed to be up for my brand of coping, so I relaxed a bit.

"They call this pose The Cleopatra," she said, forcing my back into an unnatural arch and guiding my right hand to a metal post.

"So I just lean back and give my best Elizabeth Taylor pout?"

"You got it." She laughed.

Good. If she's laughing, all is well.

"You'll get the results by mail in about a week."

When I opened the radiology report seven days later, the floor rippled under my feet, and I leaned hard into the kitchen counter.

"What is it?" My husband, Brendon, looked over my shoulder.

"'Your bilateral mammogram results show the need for further evaluation on the left breast.'" I read flatly.

He hugged me in a rich and communicative way. My husband's mother is a breast cancer survivor. This hug said, "I understand. I'm here for you. You will be okay."

Crises, small and large, reveal us. They can be gifts that show us how much we have to live for and what's really important to us. In that moment of reeling uncertainty, I was thankful for Brendon. I was also grateful for the women I knew who had stood in my shoes, faced the worst case scenario and lived—strong women I could invoke like muses to shore me up through the next series of poking and prodding and potential diagnoses. I've always sought out passionate people to share my time. Sometimes our passions save us, and that's what happened to Jeanee Bourque when she was fighting breast cancer. She was the muse I called on the most.

Art is often rendered in private. It's an act of creation and discovery that warrants soul searching and isolation, but too much alone time can often leave the artist feeling depleted and in dire need of a recharge. This need to reach out drove me to writers' conferences and book festivals. I went to the SC Book Festival to take a few seminars and meet authors who had made the move from writing for themselves to publishing their work. And that's where I met Jeanee. She was there to learn too. She was bubbly and personable and eager. We talked about writing, the craft of it and the ideas we had. She told me she was a visual artist—writing was her secondary art. For me, it was the other way around. We complemented each other well.

After the conference, we emailed and followed each other on Facebook. When I was promoting a humor book to benefit nonprofits that promote sanitation in developing countries, she came to see my first attempt at stand-up comedy. More importantly, she brought friends. So when she invited me to an art space in Lexington for a night of local music and live painting, I returned the favor. That night I was introduced to what really drives her as an artist. It was a lesson that will stay with me.

Jeanee grew up in Cape Cod and was surrounded by art and artists her entire life. Her grandfather was a professional painter in Boston who worked in oils. Jeanee's mother worked with pastels. With three brothers rough-housing outside, Jeanee often preferred to stay inside with her mom and work on arts and crafts and watercolors. As she got older, she moved on to the oils her grandfather loved before finally settling into her niche of acrylics and mixed media.

In 1995, she started to show her work publicly, and her first show was in Florida at Okaloosa College. Jeanee has had some impressive mentors in her journey, such as Guy Lipscomb, for whom she worked as a studio assistant, and Ilona Royce Smithkin. Bourque has had her work shown extensively in New York where she took lessons from Smithkin and, working as the artist's assistant, traveled with her from New York to South Carolina. Taking her cue from such a colorful character, Bourque teaches art lessons herself, with students whose ages and abilities run the gamut from toddler to centurion and novice to veteran. The beginners come to her to have fun and learn something new, but the seasoned students come to her to loosen up and shed their rigidity.

Jeanee's style is fluid. I've had the pleasure of watching Bourque's "performance art". Her signature pieces are those she paints while a local musical artist is playing live. There is a bravery and spontaneity in that act that commands respect. She takes what is traditionally produced in private, and shown after the fact, and transforms it into a shared experience. The audience becomes complicit in the art's creation because they inhabit the same space that inspires the piece. Jeanee and her audience are all listening to the same song and watching as she channels whatever the music inspires in her.

Breast cancer has not squashed her desire to create these performance-art experiences. Instead, it has increased her drive to become a better artist. When Jeanee was diagnosed she asked herself, "If I were to die what I would I miss? What would I regret?" Her college degree was in business, and while that came in handy when marketing or promoting her artistic efforts, she never pursued a degree in the field she loved. When grappling with her own mortality, art is what she realized she would miss the most, and not going to school for it was her only regret. So she enrolled in the art program at USC.

Studying art at the collegiate level introduced her to the deeper theories that informed the work of many of her favorite artists. She shared the same philosophical approach to visual art as a nonrepresentational medium. After taking a deeper look at Wassily Kandinsky, Peter Max and Miles Batt, Jeanee reevaluated what she'd like her contribution to art, and the world at large, to be. She wanted to continue to be an abstract artist.

Kandinsky's work especially had always spoken to Jeanee, but in school she learned how this forefather of abstract art saw his work as attached to music rather than objects. This was Bourque's mindset exactly. The way she paints to a piece of music as it's being played lets the music inform the art and thereby capture the intangible. The emotion evoked from the musical performance becomes something new when expressed through the painting—something abstract.

Jeanee's artistic focus is almost exclusively nonrepresentational, but cancer allowed an exception to the rule. She sketched while she was in bed with a dangerously low platelet count. Bourque's friend, who was also battling cancer, shared a visualization exercise she used to boost her own platelet count. The woman would sculpt platelet-like shapes with Play-doh while repeating the phrase, "I am making more platelets." The normal range of platelets in a healthy person is anywhere from 150,000 to 450,000 per liter of blood. At its lowest, Jeanee's count was only 20,000. Representational art as a meditative exercise in mind-over-matter was a project she undertook with the intensity and focus of a Buddhist monk. She sculpted bowls upon bowls of Play-doh platelets. Her friends rallied around the idea and made their own clay platelets in a show of solidarity. Even fighting cancer became a kind of collective performance art rooted in an emotional experience. In this case—the desire to live.

Bourque's battle with cancer, and decision to attend art school in her 40s, is an admirable example. It's a lesson we should keep present in our minds. Although we all face the same ultimate deadline, some of us are experts at forgetting. But Jeanee didn't suffer from forgetfulness: "Once you have a major scare you realize what it's like to live." And that's exactly what she's doing.

Her survival told me that I could make it even if my ultrasound revealed cancer. I took her story with me to the radiology wing of the hospital where I sat among women who waited with shared uncertainty. When the radiologist told me that he didn't see any signs of cancer, I exhaled so deeply that the world blackened at the edges. And I made my own decision. These reminders of our own mortality light existential fires under us. What would my answers to Jeanee's question be? What would I miss? What would I regret? How can I live today to answer those questions? What's stopping me from doing that right now?

We should all live in a way that faces those questions and answers them succinctly. But most of us don't. We fear rejection; we fear success. Fear is a powerful teacher, and that is the lesson I take from Jeanee Bourque. I look to her art and how it conveys the emotion of a shared moment—an intangible and visceral experience. Conveying the concrete is too cold, and Jeanee knows too well that anything concrete is fleeting anyway. The real point is to convey what sustains us, what will survive, what fuels the ghost in the machine in spite of fear.

Jeanee is in remission now, healing from one surgery and preparing for another. And I'm rooting for her and everything she stands for.

Turning "Shit" into Art: Gina Langston Brewer

By Kristine Hartvigsen

"I'm just a pick-up-shit-on-the-side-of-the-road kind of girl," Gina told me one day as we examined items tossed into the bed of her pickup truck. The morning's foraging had produced wooden drawers – not attached to a "chest of," mind you – but loose drawers of various sizes. "These can be so many things," she gushed. "I'm going to make pet beds out of them!"

I first met Gina in 1997 at the Art Bar in downtown Columbia's Vista. I'd been hosting an open mic there on Tuesday nights. Heads turned when she walked in. Everyone seemed to know this tall, striking young woman with the radiant eyes. "I'm a single mom, and I have a little boy, too!" she said as we struck up a conversation. "We should get together some time and have a picnic."

Turns out our boys were like caramel and sea salt. Although her Dylan was a couple of years older than my Colin, they bonded right away. Soon, we exchanged mother's nights out. She would sit for Colin on Tuesdays when I did open mic, and I sat for Dylan on Thursdays while she took belly dancing lessons (her desire to try new things is inexhaustible). Single moms seem never to have time for themselves. "We're mothers, not martyrs," Gina declared. It would be the beginning of a terrific circle of feminine support.

I'd never met anyone with Gina's unbridled zest for life. Early on, Colin said to me, "Gina's the coolest babysitter ever! Did you know she can steer a car with her knees!" That was Gina. Always happily doing a gazillion things at once. Her house was a warm, welcoming, wild mess, but the clutter was part of her artistic process. She saw beauty in everything – even in me. Perhaps that's why I adore her so much.

Gina had art, incense, and live plants in every room of her house. She was constantly working on several things at once. I loved that she had dirt under her fingernails and that there were paint spots on her hands.

Over the years that I've known her, Gina has been good at most any creative thing she tried. She can cook. She can sew and make the coolest hats and costumes. She can write and from time to time publishes poetry. She can sing. I was astonished to see her join her husband's band onstage at the Art Bar one weekend to sing the songs of classic country crooners. (I had no idea.) And she can act, having performed in the Vagina Monologues on more than one occasion.

While living in South Carolina, Gina showed her paintings at venues including 701 Whaley (before the renovation), Café Strudel, The Gourmet Shop, Tapp's Arts Center, and at USC-Beaufort, among other places. It is Gina's visual art that I want to focus on. I am most captivated by her paintings. To this day, they remain my favorite of her works, which span many mediums.

When we first met, Gina had just completed a lushly colored abstract Madonna-and-child. She followed that up with a series of similarly themed works. I'd never seen anything like her paintings, especially the figures. They were both curvy and geometric, simple and lavish, always bursting with vibrant color. People most often liken Gina's work to that of Picasso. Certainly the famous Spanish master and founder of the cubist movement is an influence. That's almost too easy.

"There's only one artist who inspires me." Said no artist. Ever.

Gina is an equal-opportunity art scholar. She has a fondness for art nouveau. But if you had to narrow it down, much of her work is informed by the whimsical renderings of Friedensreich Hundertwasser, a contemporary Austrian painter and architect who passed away in 2000. Another favorite is also Austrian — Gustav Klimt, perhaps best known for his iconic work, "The Kiss."

One of my favorite of Gina's abstract paintings is titled "Red Chair." It depicts a full-figured nude woman sitting on a red chair against a vivid turquoise background. The woman's skin appears nearly translucent, suggesting we can see inside her and even trace the lines of her inner parts, her deepest countenance.

I own several pieces by Gina. One is also a nude woman in shades of gold and red, and while the woman is curvy, her essence – it's not apparent whether the lines are under or over the skin – is permeated with geometric lines and angles, almost like a blueprint. I love the juxtaposition of curved and straight lines. For me, it symbolizes the duality of so many women, both the curves and the edges. I also have a portrait of a lamb that I bought at one of her shows at Tapp's. I adore its American Gothic vibe.

The "ownership" of another of Gina's paintings – a beguilingly truthful self-portrait – remains in dispute to this day. My son and I have been fighting over it for years. It originally hung in my home office. Eventually, my son wanted the office for his bedroom, and we made the switch. However he wanted me to leave the portrait behind in his "new" bedroom. I resisted. He persisted. And the painting stayed in his room. He's left the nest now and still has the painting. I've asked for it back, but he claims it's his. Part of me is happy that Gina's picture gives Colin so much pleasure. I know he loves her like a second mother. But I love the portrait, too. I'll likely have to concede to my son. I think he got his "good eye" from me.

As an education major at Winthrop College in Rock Hill, on a whim Gina enrolled in an art class. It completely changed her life. She went on to earn a master's in divergent learning from Columbia College with the goal of teaching art to the most difficult-to-teach children. And she did that, teaching art in Title One elementary schools in Richland County for a couple of years.

From the children's point of view, Gina rocked. She was the best teacher ever. She spoke their language, loved to play. She made learning fun. Perhaps most important, she showed her kids that they were important, that they mattered regardless of the harsh circumstances that often left them feeling invisible. The teaching gig did not last. One insolent principal who did not appreciate Gina's gifts crossed her at every turn, limiting her resources and generally making her life miserable. After all her hard work to make it into the classroom, Gina pondered quitting.

As the saying goes, life happens when you are busy making other plans. In 2008, Gina married the love of her life, Kevin Brewer, and they had a son, George. Within the year, Kevin, a musician and soldier, was assigned to Fort Benning in Columbus, Georgia. There Gina opened a studio, which her young son dubbed "Schoodio." Gina exhibited art and taught classes while becoming entrenched in the local art scene. She founded the Howard Avenue Art Festival and participated in many local art events, all while corralling a toddler and tending to her quirky, laying hens in the back yard.

From there, the family moved in 2013 to Fort Gordon in Augusta, where (at this writing) Gina now lives with Kevin and George. They found an ideal apartment-above-store rental space and moved in. Never idle, Gina opened the Art & Soul Corner Curio downstairs. It is not unfamiliar territory. Her mom, Karen Langston, is the longtime owner of Marketplace on Meeting, an antique and collectibles store in West Columbia. Gina finally found a hub to process all the cool stuff she picks up everywhere (including the side of the road), love it or reinvent it, and pass it along to others. She puts her eye for design to use assisting customers in finding just the right embellishment for their home to give it individual charm and whimsy.

Gina has long been inspired by her Grandmother Langston, who for as long as she can remember crafted things with found objects. At her store in Augusta, Gina creates and sells "upcycled" garden creations and repurposed furnishings, as well as all home accents and trinkets. Some of her best-sellers are repurposed light bulbs that, through Gina's eyes, are reborn as curious insects who brighten a potted plant or ceiling fan.

There's no one like Gina. She's the person on your street who's most likely to have a bottle tree. She's the friend most likely to play a didgeridoo. She inspired me to grow begonias. I will forever associate her with the heady scent of patchouli. She taught me to take time and live in the moment. I visualize her mind as a brilliant Rube Goldberg contraption cranking out endless ideas. Yeah. That's Gina. Steering with her knees and going to all the fabulous places.

An Ethereal Talent: Lynn Burgess

By Laurie Brownell McIntosh

Those who influence us and make our lives richer are not always the obvious. Sometimes they are just the new girl down the hall.

In the early 80s, perched on a crumbling concrete bench in front of the Five Points' Zesto, I looked across Blossom Street to the vacant rooms above the liquor store, wishing I could live there. Little did I know then that I would spend 15 years of my life working and creating behind those old brick walls.

In 1990, I moved my design studio into one of the funky little upstairs spaces. There were all types of tenants in and out through the early years; Insurance salesmen, restaurant owners, advocate groups, small start-ups and the most famous, Hootie and the Blowfish. As the mid 90s rolled around other artists began to move in and out... and in. Susie Scarborough worked for a while down the hall and Mary Gilkerson moved in next door. As it happens with artists, one comes, then another, and another.

I was out of the studio the better first half of 1997 with a new baby and all that goes with that job. On my return I noticed Susie had moved out and someone new had moved in. In those days I could go for weeks and not run into any of the other tenants so I was surprised when I struck out down the hall for the bathroom and ran into "the new girl."

"The new girl" sparked with a magnetic energy. She was petite with just a tufted buzz of hair covering her head. With the confidence of ten men she spun around and introduced herself. "Hi, I'm Lynne Burgess. I'm an artist and my hair is short like this because I have cancer. I'm going to be fine though." Damnedest introduction I have ever heard. A great friendship sprouted that would reshape the order of my life in this small southern city.

What I know of Lynne is limited. She was born Lynne Cox Burgess and was an army kid born in Germany. Her family eventually settled in the Conway area. She studied art at Coastal Carolina and then made her way to Columbia. She was married to Blake Burgess, a man who adored her, loved her, and understood her.

Lynne had a firm work ethic when it came to her art. She came in every day she was able and was either painting or running her framing business. There were days when she would walk up the stairs and announce to anyone near, "Today I'm going to paint my butt off."

During the years we shared these spaces Lynne worked mostly in fields of colors using oil bars on paper. These images were richly layered, abstracted, shapes and plains which she would finish off with a generous white mat and a simple black frame.

Lynne's work was solid and engaging, and her work ethic was to be admired and emulated, but the talent I admired most in her was her ability to bring people together. She collected people. Interesting people. Many a Thursday evening Lynne would open her studio and a bottle of wine and new and old faces would begin to flow in. Most were artists or collectors, but not all.

The conversations I recall best were those of art and travel and new friendships. She had a keen mind for the business and bartering side of art. She gave her knowledge and encouragement freely, and in turn others felt comfortable to do the same.

She opened my eyes, my heart, and my world to so many fascinating people that are still woven deep into the fabric of my life. Time has faded my memory but I tried to make a list of the people I met in that Blossom Street studio. On any given Thursday evening you might run into Stephen Chesley, Eileen Blyth, Mark Copeland, Bill Davis, Marcello Novo, Laura Spong or Mike and Elizabeth Williams. Dell Goodrich, Sonya Dunn and Lucy Hollingsworth were regulars, as well as the resident studio artists, Mary Gilkerson, Debra Lingle, Kathy Brown and Melissa Ligon.

I was fortunate to work and make art with Lynne for over six years in the studios that came to be known as EBCO. Our relationship was full of laughter and respect. She was very scrappy, as well. Once, when she misunderstood something I said, she threatened to "kick my ass." It would have been a tall climb up my 5'9" frame but I'm convinced she could have done it.

By 2003 I made the decision to build a home studio. My life of clients, art, meeting school buses, making snacks and carpooling kids seemed easier to control from one address. I knew I would miss my studio mates and I knew our relationships would shift and change. I attended the occasional Thursday night affair and tried to stay relevant in this group, but everyone had full and challenging lives going on in all directions. Several years later Lynne's cancer returned after a long hiatus. I saw less and less of her as she reserved her time and energy for her closest friends and family. On February 20, 2008 I got a call that Lynne had passed away.

I think about Lynne every day. I'm not quite sure why but she just pops in my head over the smallest ideas. She chirps in the back of my mind when I'm trying to decide on a frame or how I should market an upcoming show. She resonates in my mind when I think about relationships between colors and lines and shapes. I can look at one of the many treasures she brought me from her travels and it can quietly calm me before an opening reception.

I believe that the essence of our life on this earth remains until the last memory, from last person that knew us, is gone. I believe Lynne lives on through all those that she touched and brought together. She gave the gift of a trusted community to those that knew her. She gave them friendship. She gave them each other. We were all drawn to her light.

This is too short a story for too short a life. I sure wish they both could have been longer.

My Rainbow Chasing Muse: Robert Clark

By Tom Poland

If you're driving down a forgotten lane in the South Carolina countryside and you see a man in a Hawaiian shirt taking photographs, remember the scene. There's a good chance you'll see it in a book.

Come spring, Robert Clark goes afield wearing his trademark Hawaiian shirts. I know because I often accompany him.

We do books. That's our thing.

Robert and I met when we were young and naive. Robert was a quiet fellow from Charlotte who had been working as an architectural photographer. His icon was Ansel Adams, famed for his black and white photos of the American West.

I had no heroes. I was a scriptwriter and cinematographer for what's today the South Carolina Department of Natural Resources. Back then, folks knew it as the South Carolina Wildlife & Marine Resources Department. *South Carolina Wildlife* magazine was its pride and joy, its flagship. Robert had come onboard as a photographer. That told me all I needed to know about his abilities. In its heyday, the magazine had few rivals when it came to stellar photography.

Despite working for bureaucrats with the vision of a star-nosed mole, John Culler had managed to turn a flimsy black-and-white flyer into a full-color conservation magazine, the country's best. A bearded, lanky Georgian with a gunslinger's cool demeanor, he could have been Josey Wales. He gave me my break as a writer, hiring me to write film scripts. Were it not for Culler, Robert Clark and I would have never met. Were it not for Culler, we would not have co-authored books and scores of features.

On Robert's first day on the job his boss took him on the requisite introduction tour. Later, in private, I told Robert we should go to lunch so I could give him the lay of the land. Our section of South Carolina Wildlife was a snake pit of egos, absurd rules, and turf wars, a deadly brew with a pinch of pettiness thrown in for good measure. It could do in a creative fellow. That was 1982. Robert and I went to lunch at Tony's on Washington Street where I told him who was dangerous and who wasn't. We became friends.

It wasn't long before Robert was garnering more than his share of covers. Talent is a beautiful burst of rainbow-colored steam; you can't hold it in. Two years after he joined the magazine, I became its managing editor. For four years, I assigned and wrote features but our opportunities to collaborate were few. He did his thing and I did mine. Meanwhile, I was teaching at night, freelancing, and growing weary of bureaucrats. The bullshit, mean-spirited people, and lack of creative challenge were killing my soul. I felt like a lost man in a lost world. In 1986, Robert sensed I was about to quit. In an act of kindness, he took me aside. "Before you leave, why don't we go out one morning and drive a back road until we see something we both like. We'll do a story on it."

We set out one spring day around 8:00 A.M. seeking something meaningful. Down Highway 378, we found it: the vanishing shanties of a vanishing South. The first hint of our alchemy produced a classic feature, "Tenant Homes—A Testament

To Hard Times." Newspapers and journals reprinted it, and it caught the eye of the acquisitions editor at the University of South Carolina Press, Warren Slesinger. He had been planning a book on South Carolina's natural areas with a colleague, Steve Bennett. Warren set up a lunch with the three of us at the old Carolina Hotel. He was putting a team together.

"You fellows are going to do a book," he said. The book was *South Carolina—The Natural Heritage* with a foreword by James Dickey. Robert's act of compassion and creativity had pointed my life in a new direction. Robert Clark, had, in fact, saved my creative life. Following *The Natural Heritage*, which focused on pristine habitat and endangered species, we turned to our theme, forgotten backroads. *South Carolina—A Timeless Journey* resulted and later came *Reflections Of South Carolina*, a book still in print with approximately 35,000 copies sold. And now *Reflections Of South Carolina, Vol. 2* should eclipse *Reflections*. All books can trace their ancestry to that spring day we drove a state truck down Highway 378 looking for a story to tell. Since then, we have been to many nooks and crannies in the state seeking that certain "something we both like."

It astounds us that no others do what we do. I asked Jonathan Haupt, director of the University of South Carolina Press, if he knew of another writer-photographer team that does what we do. "No," he said. We suspect that's because it is harder work than it appears. We pretty much live with our subject matter, just as Walker Evans and James Agee lived with poor families.

We see ourselves as preservationists. Much of what we document in our books will soon be gone. Old tobacco barns crumble. Fire towers fall. Windmills topple, and ways of life have a way of disappearing, but the pivotal thing here—the reason for this piece—is what Robert Clark means to my work. His vision, patience, and calm demeanor do good things for me. On our road trips, we share thoughts, memories, frustrations, and perspectives. The stuff life's made of.

We never cross swords, something unusual among co-authors. "What's there to fight about," says Robert. He's right. How many get the privilege of doing what we do?

We've paid our dues with jobs and assignments too painful to waste ink on. We're grateful to do what we do and we thank destiny for bringing us together at the end of a long road. I remember Robert's telling me the moment light captivated him. He had to catch the school bus before daybreak. Peering through a window, a 12-year-old saw fire and smoke pouring from chimneys against a pink sky. That moment would drive his study of the language of light. For me it was getting honorable mention in a Father's Day essay contest when I was nine. The die for each was cast.

Robert's taught me the value of preparation and patience. He's a scholar of the sky and weather. When you see one of his unforgettable images it's not a lucky shot. In *Reflections Of South Carolina* and *Reflections Of South Carolina, Vol. II*, Lowcountry photographs illustrate what I mean. It's no coincidence that high tide and a rising moon (crystal clear because of the low humidity forecast) fill the page in his "Hunting Island Moonrise" nor is it good luck that that "Fripp Inlet Moonrise Setting Sun" captures the moon setting in the west as the sun rises. This rare photo in late September fools viewers into believing the sun is rising beneath the moon. Its pink and aqua sky and crepuscular rays serve a feast to the eyes. He scouted the shots and anticipated conditions.

He has what I deem the Vision of Glittering Potential, an intuition for splendor. He teaches me to see the world not as it is but as it can be. One fall afternoon we were walking through woods talking. When he didn't answer a question, I turned to see him 20 yards back staring up into a tree.

"See that swirl of color there?"

I saw colored leaves, nothing more. When the photograph came out, there it was, a swirling DNA-like helix of color.

"You don't take a photograph. You make it." Ansel Adams said that, words that most assuredly resonate with Robert.

Our collaborations have taken us out of South Carolina. We spent four days in Winter Haven, Florida, covering the 60th anniversary of Cypress Gardens for a national magazine. We travel well and it is on the road that we discuss art without sounding like academics or dreamy-eyed fools. We believe the silliness of dressing "like an artist" in no way makes you legit. We shun the affectations of an artist. When we're invited to book signings we joke that we should don berets, wear an eye patch, slap on a fake goatee, and act haughty. "Please! Be quiet. We are creating!" Then we have a big laugh. Your work speaks with more eloquence than any image you gin up.

He teaches me that art emerges at its own rate. For a long time he has pursued the peerless rainbow and it was that quest that inspired the conclusion to my somewhat autobiographical novel. I based a character, Cameron, the Rainbow Chaser, on him in *Forbidden Island*. In this tale, a beleaguered Atlanta writer on his way to the last wild island stops in Columbia to enlist the help of the best photographer he's worked with.

> My first stop would be in Columbia to see Cameron, a man who approached photography with a purity born of art ... Cameron knew the Lowcountry and its swamps, rivers, and people, and he was honest. He would prepare me for whatever awaited. Like all true artists, he had his own mission—the once-in-a-lifetime rainbow.

Rainbows are difficult subjects, predictable, nonetheless ephemeral, but a garden's easy, right? It never moves, and light aplenty feeds it. Well no, a garden necessitates an ambitious effort artistically. The photographer must capture mood because a garden reflects the lives and dreams of those who nurture it. Robert Clark understands this. He's fluent in the language of light and his eloquence informs my work. Sometimes when a feature or essay isn't going right, I look at our books. It's inspiring to see beauty that otherwise would be lost had we not bothered to cover it. Take, for instance, the photograph on pages 86 and 87 of *Reflections of South Carolina*. You see this fine reddish, rusting roof on an old barn. The sky is blue and behind the barn grows a lustrous crop of golden canola. The barn is old. I doubt it's standing today but the canola signifies a new start. On that same spread is an old windmill at sunset. An era dies right before your eyes.

Robert has done good things for my career, but perhaps the best was his honest advice to get out from behind my desk.

"You do your best work in the field," he told me. "When you get out, your writing is so much more alive."

He's right.

One morning long ago, Robert and I were driving down Highway 378, and it changed our life. Since then, we've logged thousands of miles all over South Carolina and the South. I have gained from him creative patience, a vision for preservation, the ability to see beauty in the simplest things, and a mutual alchemy that turns the commonest subjects into gold. In full disclosure I must say this: he is a better photographer than I am a writer. I rode his coattails the world of books. Had it not been for his advice and art, I'd be a nobody. It's up to me now not to blow it.

Deceptive, destructive people have come into my life crushing me with their heaviness. Robert's pure acts of creation, like ravishing birthday balloons, lifted me above

Were it not for my Rainbow Chasing Muse, the man in the Hawaiian shirt, my writing would be all the poorer and it needs all the help it can get. As James Dickey told me, "None of us are good writers. We don't live long enough."

Robert might say that's true of photographers too, but he's the exception, not the rule. Of that I am certain.

And Then She Gave Me a Song: Deborah Deck

By Debra Daniel

In 1961, everything was changing. Kennedy exuded youth and energy, a new kind of President who had challenged citizens to give something of themselves to their country. The Civil Rights Movement steamed its heat throughout the South. A current of hope sizzled, but with it traveled a deeper undercurrent of fear. My family, generally non-political, didn't discuss or debate those issues around the dinner table so what I knew was from classmates who had overheard swirls of their own parents' conversations. They whispered that black children might be in our classrooms, that there'd be a lot of trouble if that happened. For us kids, those scary adult issues disappeared when the talk turned to summer birthday parties and swimming pools and wondering who would be our fifth grade year teacher. In 1961, what mattered to me was that I turned 10 years old and was ready for my own changes.

Already my Mother had taken me to buy my first training bra, really nothing more than an abbreviated undershirt, but wearing it filled me with grown up pride. I'd had my hair set at a beauty salon in a style like Annette Funicello and competed in the Little Miss Maid of Cotton Contest as one of twenty-five finalists where I lost miserably, finishing behind lots of frilly giggling girls who had polished their pivot and curtsy and knew how to show off their dimples and curls. Still I assured myself that, had there been a talent competition, a category in which I was certain I'd soar, I would've glided away with the crown so I vowed that when my next opportunity came, I'd be ready to fling myself into the larger world. I knew exactly how I'd do it.

I started to beg, but it wasn't for tap dancing lessons. Not a tutu and toe shoes either. And definitely not piano. No, I wanted to sing and not just as an ordinary member of the children's choir. I yearned for bigger. From as far back as I could remember I'd considered myself a singer. My Mother had told everyone how, at three, I'd asked her if I was singing with personality. At 10, I was quite proud of my repertoire and belted out tunes from, "Lipstick on Your Collar" to "Tea for Two," from "Won't You Come Home, Bill Bailey" to "The Lord's Prayer." In the mirror, I practiced singing commercials. I memorized lyrics from Broadway musicals, sang along with the albums so that on road trips, my family would be captive audience to entire scores. At home, I produced my own shows, forcing my sisters to be backup singers. I dreamed I'd be a great entertainer, a headliner, a showstopper. That would take hard work, but I was willing to learn so I begged and pleaded. For. Voice. Lessons. I pestered and badgered. Finally, my Mother said yes. That was how I met Deborah Deck.

A family friend had given us her name and phone number. My Mother probably hoped Deborah Deck would say that voice lessons for a child would be a waste of money, but to my delight, she accepted me. Voila, just like that, I had a teacher. And not just any teacher. To my girlish eyes, Deborah Deck stood gloriously beautiful. I had no idea that she'd graduated summa cum laude from Indiana University where she earned her Bachelor and Master of Music degrees. I didn't know she was a classically trained opera singer and pianist, or that she'd studied under professionals from the Metropolitan Opera in New York and had toured professionally as a lyric soprano throughout the United States and Europe. Those details reflect a vision of the accomplished, complex woman she was, but I wouldn't discover that until, recently when I started searching for her on the Internet.

My childish view was narrower in scope and substance. It was enough for me to see Deborah Deck as a whirling presence with the power to uplift and liberate my singing. I was ready for her to transform me. She possessed an aura both serene and commanding, both regal and gentle, radiating Southern charm and hospitality that made me feel welcome and at ease, but there was something about her poise and confidence that I couldn't define, something expansive and more worldly. To me, she appeared as a magical blend of fairy godmother/Miss America/guardian angel/enchantress. In her own living room of her own elegant house stood a baby grand piano. How miraculous. A baby grand piano. It seemed Liberace would enter at any moment. I didn't know real people in Columbia, South Carolina, had such things in their own houses, but each week I stood in the curve of a piano so superbly polished that I could see my own reflection, and I gazed at Deborah Deck as she allowed me to open my voice and sing.

My lesson every Thursday afternoon granted complete bliss. My Mother would drop me off and I'd sit on the front porch steps until the piano student ahead of me was finished. Then Deborah Deck opened her door for me. She smelled of peppermint and wore fitted shirtwaist dresses with billowy skirts, modest but infinitely suitable for twirling. Everything about her was perfect. Her hair, softly dark and shiny, framed her face in little dips and swirls as she watched me with alert and knowing eyes that penetrated and gleamed with intelligence. I was not accustomed to such willing and unwavering attention for such an uninterrupted span of time. I'd always been one of a trio of sisters, one of a choir, one of a classroom full of nondescript children, but in the spotlight of Deborah Deck's living room, I stood solo.

She taught me how to care about my voice, the importance of vocalizing and the power of breathing from my diaphragm. She emphasized enunciation and showed me how to place my notes and tones strategically inside my mouth, how to move smoothly from my head voice to my chest. She taught with such ease, making it seem so natural and nonchalant, that I didn't even realize I was learning.

Weeks passed along into autumn, bringing the usual changes as leaves colored and fell and limbs and branches became more clearly defined. I was changing, too, discovering the colors in my voice, from delicate pink, to the bright clarity of silver, to burgundy rich and dark. Deborah Deck was showing me how to project, to lift my song into the air so that it would flow and linger not only in quiet, empty corners, but also resonate through an entire auditorium, so that it would settle not only into the listeners' ears, but also into their collective consciousness. And she did this with seemingly innocuous Halloween songs and the nonsense syllables of vocal exercises.

And then she gave me a song. A new piece of sheet music always promised a thrill, another rite of passage. It meant that Deborah Deck thought I was ready for a something better, something harder, something she believed I could make my own. This song would be one of the most important songs I'd ever sing. It was called, "Stay in Your Own Backyard." The melodic line played sweet and lilting almost a lullaby, soothing and sleepy. At first listen, as she sang it to me, the tune seemed easy enough, but, in truth, it proved challenging in its range and nuance of intervals. Still it only took a few minutes before I was singing along.

But there was a larger lesson that week, a lot larger. The lyrics told the story of a little black boy shunned by white children. He'd come home weeping because none of them would play with him. His Mother nestled him onto her lap to comfort him, it seemed, but what she told him was that he should stay in his own backyard. His own Mother told him to stay on his side of the fence, that he shouldn't expect anything different from white children. In the second verse the boy dies, his sad little face gone forevermore. Still his Mother sat in her rocker and sang the same refrain, "Stay in your own backyard."

Deborah Deck gave me a song that touched me, a song that broke my heart. I couldn't imagine such meanness would be real, and I couldn't imagine the sorrowful resignation of the boy and, even more so, of his mother, that they had to accept such isolation and injustice merely because their skin was a different color. Week after week, Deborah Deck and I worked on that song. She told me to feel the words, to let my emotions show on my face and blend them into my singing, and to let the purity and clearness of my notes and tones move from deep inside of me.

Whenever I sang that song I noticed the room became still, almost airless. Her eyes and my own would always fill. In the curve of that shiny piano, I saw my reflection. I was one of those white children, but, surely, I'd be different. Wouldn't I? I didn't know any black children, but like my classmates I'd been afraid of what might happen if they came to our school. Weren't they just kids after all, and probably just as scared? Would I have the courage to be kind to them?

I'd like to say I changed instantly, but I was a 10 year-old girl growing up in the South. It would take years for my beliefs and perspectives to solidify, but Deborah Deck had planted the seed. Everyone knows the arts and the artists who create them have tremendous influence on people and society. Paintings, books, symphonies, even a single piece of sheet music can inspire, evoke, persuade, and sometimes take a person to a different place than was intended. That's how "Stay in Your Own Backyard," impacted me.

Recently, I searched for it on the Internet, too. Written in 1899, it was indicative of many songs of the era that promoted prejudice and stereotypes, clearly meant to keep people segregated and in their places. The words are so cringe worthy and racially charged, it would never be sung in public today, but I still remember every word. It's deeply embedded in my memory and still elicits in me the same desire to weep for that little boy and his mother.

I believe Deborah Deck chose that song for me with a purpose beyond its pleasant melody and plaintive lyric, but I'll never know for sure. After only a year as her student, she moved to another city. I never saw her again. Deborah Deck passed away in 2011, but I found her obituary on the Internet. It tells me a lot, these lines especially. "It was in her nature to make those in her presence feel unequivocally welcomed, for she genuinely valued and respected others, making sure no one felt like an outsider. As open was her door, so were her mind and heart."

I wish I'd searched for Deborah Deck sooner. I would've told her I sang the lead in my high school musical, was selected for All State Chorus, and that I continued to sing in musical theater and as church soloist, in weddings and funerals and that, now, fifty years after she was my first teacher, I sing more than ever in a several bands alongside my husband. Surely she would've been pleased.

Deborah Deck inspired me to be a better singer, to feel the music and the words, to give them meaning beyond a mere string of notes on a staff. I'm grateful for that, but I'm more appreciative that she taught me bigger lessons. She'll never know how often I've told others about that song and about her, and about how she helped me see beyond my own small reflection, giving me a clearer view to a world larger than myself.

A Vital Force: Cynthia Gilliam

By August Krickel

This is how I picture her: a striking young woman in her twenties, zooming down a rural Southern highway in a sporty red convertible. She may be wearing sunglasses; she may be wearing a scarf that merrily trails behind her like a banner, as the wind tosses it this way and that. Her hair is fashionably short, like the stars of the day – Audrey Hepburn, or Twiggy, and her strong chin and serene countenance might remind one a little of the young Julie Andrews.

It's the 1960s, and she is already a success in what was then a man's world. She's at the top of her game both professionally and artistically, with an impossibly fulfilling life and career still ahead of her. She looks hopeful, and carefree, and fearless.

I never saw any such moment, of course. I would have been not much more than a toddler then, and didn't meet Cynthia Gilliam until decades later, but she has described this image to me many times. In those days, she worked in radio, later becoming a fabulously successful advertising executive. Corporate accomplishments aside, Gilliam made a much greater and ultimately more enduring contribution to the Midlands: with a few colleagues (or perhaps co-conspirators) she changed the face of local theatre forever.

Her adventures began innocuously. Spending her early years in the small towns of Carlisle and Whitmire, Gilliam moved into a home on Laurens Street when her family relocated to Columbia. She had a little gang of friends, including the late Jim E. Quick, who lived nearby on Wheeler Hill. I imagine them at 11 or 12 meeting for ice cream sodas somewhere in Five Points, then bicycling over to Kawana Road where they took acting classes with Mary Lou Kramer. Kramer, who taught drama at Columbia College and headed the children's program at Town Theatre, also gave private lessons, producing plays in her backyard Playhouse Studio. Several generations of local actors learned their craft from Kramer, most then going on to roles at Town Theatre.

The nation's oldest continuosly operating community theatre, Town for nearly half a century brought in the best and the brightest from top schools like Yale, recent MFA graduates who stayed for a few years as resident director before moving on to Broadway or Hollywood. Gilliam recalls how "wealthy, well-traveled, well-educated people" on the Board of Governors were familiar with and naturally expected professional-caliber performances. Clad in formal attire, they treated casts to elegant opening night receptions even for the children's shows, and followed up the next day with handwritten thank you notes. As a teen, Gilliam found an affinity for character roles; among her favorites were the Witch in *Hansel and Gretel*, an evil stepsister in *Cinderella*, and especially the Wicked Witch of the West in *The Wizard of Oz*, in which her performance was aided by special pyrotechnic effects from friend Christian Thee, later technical director at Town and now an acclaimed visual artist.

Although majoring in journalism at USC, and pulling double duty in shows at Drayton Hall on campus and across Sumter Street at Town, Gilliam wanted to build up professional credits to earn an Equity card, and did two seasons of summer stock at the Hill Top Theatre in Baltimore, where Thee had interned earlier. Her eyes twinkle as she recalls playing a stripper in *Pal Joey*, noting that she "certainly had never done that before, and my mother was hundreds of miles away." Midway through that second summer, she and her castmates had gone to dinner after their performance, and enjoyed a burlesque show to which they had received free tickets. Piling into one crowded car afterwards, Gilliam reclined across the laps of the young men in the back seat, and I can hear the exuberant giggles of young actors out for a night on the town. Then brakes screeched, the car hit another, and Gilliam's face was slammed into an ash tray on the back of the front seat. She was fortunate to be in a city with excellent medical facilities, and reconstructive surgery on her nose left no visible damage, but her mother arrived and announced that it was time to come home to Columbia.

The next summer she successfully auditioned for another regional theatre, but realized that roles available to a 21-year-old ingénue would be limited to the very bottom tier of the professional acting world. She was accustomed to doing serious leads by now - the title role in Shaw's *St. Joan,* Annie in *The Miracle Worker*, Cecily in *The Importance of Being Earnest,* and Stella in *A Streetcar Named Desire.* I look at a photo from that last one, as Stanley clings to her in a moment of vulnerability; even in a 50-year-old still photo, her expression still at once conveys power and compassion, strength, nurturing, and forgiveness. With a viable new degree in journalism, Gilliam had other options, and ended up as a copywriter at WOIC radio, developing PSA's, thanks to a connection with the station owner through community theatre. She rose to Corporate Director for Public Affairs and Traffic for Speidel Broadcasters, supervising six stations in the southeast, traveling in that red company convertible.

And of course she acted. Local audiences and critics loved her. A review of *St. Joan* at Town Theatre in 1960 describes her performance as "captivating. Her presence is undeniable. She exhibited the results of faithful study of her character...she showed a remarkable flexibility and a rewarding vocal ease. There was a refreshing honesty which she brought to the part, a quality which is sometimes lost in performances by more mature dramatic actresses."

The 1960s were a time of rebellion, a time when young people were asserting themselves, and time when women were coming to prominence everywhere. With colleagues (and friends from theatre) Mary Arnold Garvin and Elinor Pettit, Gilliam struck out on her own and opened Semaphore, the little ad agency known for the multi-colored flags decorating its exterior, which grew to become one of Columbia's largest, most prolific, and most successful. Years of connections to business leaders who supported and/or dabbled in theatre led to word-of-mouth referrals and networking, and soon Gilliam had major clients and national exposure. She recalls a meeting with the head of Richtex Brick, who bluntly asked "You're a woman - I'm selling bricks. What do you know about that?" "Give me two weeks," she said, returning with an entire campaign of billboard ads that went on to win a national award.

That same fearlessness spilled over into Gilliam's artistic life. With solid, rigorous training from Mary Lou Kramer, she and Jim E. Quick were eager to direct their own shows. "We were on fire back in the day," Gilliam recalls. "There were no limits - we could do whatever we pleased to do as long as we were willing and able to pay the bills we incurred." Gypsies, they staged shows like *Who's Afraid of Virginia Woolf* in borrowed venues including Safran's Antique Gallery on Gervais and the former Eau Claire Post Office building. They produced a well-attended, well-reviewed season of dinner theatre shows at the Laurel Hill

Supper Club, including everything from *Dracula* to lesser known Tennessee Williams plays like *This Property is Condemned* and *Period of Adjustment*. No one told them, however, that patron's second visit to the dinner buffet incurred a second charge from the restaurateur; profits disappeared, and they closed after one season. But people were watching, and taking note.

Although groups such as the Hadassah Players and the Lyric Opera staged periodic productions in school auditoriums, and both Columbia College and USC had active drama programs, Town Theatre was still in many ways the only game in town. When a popular resident director's contract was not renewed, many younger performers, frustrated by the organization's perceived leadership by non-actor socialites and businessmen, decided the time had come for a new theatre. A director‹s theatre, created in the spirit of protest and experimentation of the era, where management and play selection was driven by actors and hands-on volunteers. After an initial fund-raising revue, the newly-christened Workshop Theatre debuted in 1968 with Dylan, directed by Kramer, and starring Quick and Gilliam. Not yet 30, Gilliam earned this praise from critic Adger Brown: "It has long been this reviewer's wan hope to see Cynthia Gilliam perform badly - a hope born not of malice, but only because it is disconcerting to encounter a performer who, no matter what the role, never falters, never misses a theatrical trick, who knows exactly what she is doing - and who does it brilliantly." He concluded that this "inspired and compelling characterization" was "another personal triumph for Miss Gilliam."

A Who's Who of local talent joined her at the new Workshop Theatre, which followed Gilliam's model of performing in borrowed venues, including the Art Museum auditorium, and a small theatre at Fort Jackson. She directed Garvin and Malie Heider as Blanche and Stella in Streetcar for Workshop's third production, then directed Quick as Pseudolus in *A Funny Thing Happened on the Way to the Forum*, featuring Columbia's first racially diverse cast. Quick directed a show that season too: *Peter Pan*, which I saw at age 8. Just about anyone who was a rising young talent in town performed at Workshop: Pam Inabinet Bailey, Bette Herring, Jim O'Shea, Ann Dreher, Beth Burnside, Drucilla Brookshire, Johnny DeHart, Gerald Floyd, Jim Thigpen, Lou and Hazel Kaplan and their daughter Kay. Taking over and renovating a former dance school on the Museum property, Workshop produced *Oedipus* with Greek masks, *The Boys in the Band* when gay-themed plays were taboo, *Godspell* when it was deemed sacrilegious, as well as straightforward renditions of everything from *Macbeth*, to *Sleuth*, *The Glass Menagerie* to *The Music Man* (outdoors at Sesquicentennial State Park.) Gilliam directed one or more plays every year, occasionally returning to acting in the title roles in *The Prime of Miss Jean Brodie* and *I Remember Mama*. While Gilliam felt that she was wrong for the role of Mama (and ended up in the emergency room after throwing out her back while lifting a child actor) Jackie Brooks' review included this: "Cynthia Gilliam is utterly convincing as Mama, so believable that she forces you to forget her other identity, and to accept her as the person she portrays. And make no mistake, she is the star of this piece."

Workshop expanded into a new 199-seat facility, and Gilliam continued as mainstay into the 1990s, directing, serving as board president, even reprising her role in *Dylan* for its 20th anniversary. An increasingly successful business executive, she drew corporate contacts in as theatre benefactors, using her professional skills in advertising to design award-winning flyers, posters, programs, and marketing tools. She was a pioneer in collaboration among disciplines: the first board president of the new Columbia City Ballet at age 24, she often was listed as director for ballet performances, with Ann Brodie credited as choreographer. In other words, she handled the instruction in the pantomiming of feeling and emotion, a subject she later taught to USC theatre students. She confesses to being fascinated by dance as an expressive form, after taking six weeks of movement classes in college when a director advised her that she walked on stage like a plow horse. Brodie often returned the favor, choreographing many Workshop shows, including the horse movements for Gilliam's production of *Equus*.

Why was she so successful as a director? Gilliam gives all credit to her mentor Mary Lou Kramer, and patterns her style after her. "Everybody knows what they are going to be doing at what time, at what date, and where, from the first rehearsal. And I block the way she did. (Although) I move people more often than she did. In a play like *Virginia Woolf*, where things begin rather congenially... then you begin to move people, not necessarily getting up and walking around, but moving them on chairs and sofas to indicate agitation and rising emotion and so forth." Bill Starr wrote in a 1985 review of *Agnes of God* from 1985 that "Ms. Gilliam has directed with an authority that is belied by the smoothness of the production. She moves characters on and off stage with perfectly framed motion, and she draws emphasis to and from them with understanding that enhances meaning. A director's role is often not properly noticed in a production where so many things are working well, but Ms. Gilliam›s work here deserves special mention for its assurance and stage knowledge."

Barbara Lowrance Hughes has acted in many Gilliam-helmed plays, from *Steel Magnolias* in the 1980s to *The Dixie Swim Club* in 2011, and says that Gilliam "always has a beautifully clear vision of any play she directs, and can communicate her vision to the actors, designers and crew in a way that few directors can. She has the uncanny ability to get inside the minds of her actors and help them to see and feel the roles they are playing, so that they can 'become' that character in a deeply personal way. She always demands the very best work from her cast and crew, and she does it with kindness, caring, and a true sense of joy and play. She has been a wonderful mentor and friend to me, and I'd walk over hot coals to do anything she asks me to do!" Leigh Stevenson echoes this sentiment: "Cynthia is an actor's actor and actor's director. Her ability to see and feel the play as a piece of art is legendary."

While I've done shows with Hughes and Stevenson (directed by Quick) I never got the chance to work with Gilliam. I auditioned, once, for *Noises Off*, making it as far as callbacks. The character I was reading for spends part of the show with his trousers down around his ankles, as part of a farcical play-within-a-play. I decided I could impress the director by doing this during the reading, and so came prepared with gym shorts under my khakis. Alas, another actor, similar in age, build and type had the same idea. He read first, dropped his pants, and I knew if I did the same thing it would look as if I were simply copying him. He was cast, but all ended well, as I got plenty of laughs a couple of blocks around the corner at Town as Uncle Jocko and Mr. Goldstone in *Gypsy,* while Cynthia's actors were nearly breaking their necks in her rapid choreography for that extremely fast-paced show. As a writer, I reviewed many of her productions, including Gurney's *The Perfect Party*. Jim E. Quick and the rest of the cast did a great job, and the pace was superb, but I was not wild about the material, and my editor ran the review with the headline "A Perfect Production of a Bad Play." Hopefully she has forgiven me.

As her business thrived and boomed in the 1990s, Gilliam led by example and devoted less time to activities outside work. Then, at an age when many would be looking ahead to retirement, she and her partner decided to become parents. "Why not have it all?" she explains. "If you want it, and you can. I was living with and in love with someone who had the same goal as I did." At which point she took a long break from theatre, not wanting to miss a single moment in her new daughter's young life. Retiring in 2012, Gilliam says of her advertising career "I loved it - some of the best fun I ever had in my life. I got to travel, and meet people who were entrepreneurs and were doing remarkable things."

Gilliam seems reserved at first, if you don't know her, but when I run into her with former castmates like Lowrance Hughes and Stevenson at The Mousetrap on trivia nights, she's one of the girls, as they giggle at each other's jokes, and squeal with glee when their team gets a question right. Only when the topic of her first child, Workshop Theatre, arises, does she become sad, and her voice cracks with emotion. Workshop never owned their property, after decades of superlative performances, the building was demolished as she and I discussed this very piece, to make way for a new Law School; Workshop now rents space for shows. "Heartbroken" is the word she most often uses, but she's not dwelling in the past. Indeed, as her now-teenage daughter grew older, Gilliam returned to directing, first at Town, then Workshop, and now plans to develop her own brand, independently producing shows just as she did with Quick almost half a century ago. She reads new plays, she sees new plays, she asks for recommendations on new works and new venues. Yet at the same time, she acknowledges the current economy's toll on the arts, creating an environment where most of the great works of drama are neglected, in favor of pop hits at the box office.

Cynthia Gilliam directed more shows than anyone at Workshop, save for Jim E. Quick and Ann Dreher (who only surpassed her by a couple each.) More than a prolific and universally-acclaimed director and performer, though, I think it is her vision that will be seen as her greatest contribution to theatre in the Midlands. With Quick, she was the first to stage credible shows on her own, not as part of some larger group. Having worked with the beloved Quick on two shows, I'm sure he wouldn't have done it on his own. Together, however, they were unstoppable, and their reputation gave credibility to Workshop as an alternative to what had gone before. Their talent then ensured that Workshop's quality mirrored its ambition. Seeing their success, an entire generation of theatre folks realized "Wait a minute - we could actually do that!" From there Jim and Kay Thigpen realized they could found Trustus. From there suburban groups in Lexington, Chapin, and West Columbia realized that they too could start their own performing groups. Niches were there to be filled, for children›s productions, outdoor productions, Shakespearean productions, ethnic-centric productions.

Ultimately, it all stems from the audacity of Gilliam and Quick, two twenty-somethings who grew up together and bonded over a love of performing. Mary Lou Kramer and Town Theatre begat Cynthia Gilliam, and she begat the vital performing community we have today. And she's still here. She's still a vital force. You know, I think Cynthia Gilliam's best work just might still lie ahead of her.

A Gentle Southern Voice: Bentz Kirby

By James D. McCallister

One afternoon about ten years ago, the phone rang at the Deadheady retail store my wife Jenn and I own. A musician by night, she'd been recruited to perform alongside other locals at an anti-Iraq war rally featuring the eloquent and touchingly bereaved Army mom Cindy Sheehan. A big crowd was expected, from both protesters of the war as well as counter-protesters—this is an Army town, after all.

But the sentiments and winds were shifting, especially in the university neighborhood where we work. As the Iraq occupation started to drag on, we'd begun to sell almost as many anti-Bush and pro-peace stickers as we did for the Grateful Dead and Phish.

Problem was that some dude named 'Vince' had come out from under some rock, claiming to be a musician and wanting to perform at the rally. He'd called a number of times and left messages. At the time, neither of us knew who he was.

When the phone buzzed, the caller ID showed that number. Again. I said with a sigh, "It's that Vince guy."

"No, I think he said it's 'Bentz, with a B and a Z." Earlier, Jenn had pretended to be an employee. Had taken the message herself. A little trick we pull on telemarketers and reps.

I questioned her interpretation of the spelling, but went with it. Said, I'll handle this. "Ah," I answered. "The infamous 'Bentz'."

A gentle Southern voice, inflected with quiet and careful humility, responded. "Well now, I don't want to be infamous."

At the time I didn't know how cool of a cat Bentz Kirby would turn out to be, but honestly all this reluctance had more to do with being in the sales trade, where you learn to vibrate at a frequency of 'negatory' to most all phone solicitations, even ones as ostensibly harmless as a guitar picker looking for a gig.

To wit: Bentz/Vince expressed a heartfelt interest in playing the Sheehan appearance, to which I listened and went mm-hm.

You can guess the rest—I received his entreaties about playing, but remained noncommittal. Begged off by saying, not only do we not know who you are, I don't handle the booking, I'll pass your message along, et cetera. It was true enough. Neither Jenn nor I were organizers of the event.

Didn't think any more of it, attended the rally, and all went well, except for arguing with a couple of patriotic flag-snapping military fetishists intent on persuading me that whether WMD had been found didn't matter, that Saddam had gotten everything he deserved for attacking us on 9/11. Good times.

For all I know, Bentz Kirby himself might have been in attendance that night, but I don't remember meeting him. In due time, however, I'd discover what a wonderful soul and close friend—a best friend, eventually—he'd become to me, this anonymous guitar picker to whom I'd given an indifferent, shrugging cold shoulder.

———

Thus began my association with the inestimable Richard Bentz Kirby, a friend who has meant the world to me on a personal level, but who also stands as a veritable pillar of Columbia's music community, especially in the realm of Americana and traditional music. His star shines bright on the stages he graces.

So, too, do those of the sidemen and -women who populate his bands Alien Carnival and Jellyroll & Delicious Dish, and the musicians at the open mic nights he hosts who brave the lone soulless microphone stand, a microphone stand that's not a fellow human being filled with empathy and solidarity, but a cold and clinical tool, a device, through which the artist may project a depiction of his soul. That's what music is, after all, and whether he's singing or encouraging fellow musicians to spread their wings onstage alongside him, that's what Bentz Kirby does: reveals a glimmer of the mysterious life-stoked creative fire that drives the creative artist to ply his trade.

———

Like millions of people his age—a true American baby boomer, he's now 60—Bentz's interest in music goes back to his initial exposure to songs by artists like Bob Dylan, the Beatles, and the Byrds.

"I can remember the first time I heard [The Byrds' version of] 'Mr. Tambourine Man,' in about the fifth or sixth grade. I was in the lobby of the YMCA in Easley playing bumper pool, and it was just a very strange and different sound."

His interest became further stoked by seminal rock records such as Sgt. Pepper's Lonely Hearts Club Band, as well as a once-invaluable resource on which the iPod-generation no longer relies in the quest to discover interesting music: the radio.

"An old FM station, WQOK, had a lot of influence on me. In one hour you could hear everything from the Beatles to Patti Page to Sinatra to Motown soul music to Johnny Horton."

As an older teenager, his introduction to large scale live music included several famous concerts of the era. The West Palm Beach International Music and Arts Festival featured superstars Janis Joplin, Jefferson Airplane, and the Rolling Stones, as well as relative unknowns such as King Crimson and Grand Funk Railroad.

"On Sunday the Vanilla Fudge played, then Johnny Winter, then Janis—they all came out and jammed."

That next summer, his musical journey included two important events: First, a daylong Atlanta concert called the Cosmic Carnival, at which he saw acts like Frank Zappa and Traffic, as well as a new group that made an impression, the Allman Brothers Band. A month later came the "Southern Woodstock" known as the Atlanta International Pop Festival, where, along with superstars like Jimi Hendrix, he again saw the Allman Brothers, for whom he had cultivated true admiration.

But the more music he absorbed, the more he wished to make his own.

For all his youthful interest in music, however, a long lapse would come between his initial fantasies about writing and performing, and his status as an elder statesman of the Columbia music scene. "As an adolescent, I wanted to be a rock star, not a lawyer."

As John Lennon once said, however, life sometimes gets in the way of our dreams. Law school, a practice, a house, a family. Music would have to wait for act two of his life.

———

All was to change, though, because of another source of music in many people's lives—the church he attended. He'd done some singing with the choir, getting his bearings by listening to the other voices; because he had a guitar, he was asked to play in a praise and worship band.

A church talent show, however, was his first true stab at singing and playing in public. "I was planning to do Bob Dylan's 'Every Grain of Sand,' and right about the same time I had been trading email with Roger McGuinn," one of the voices from The Byrds who'd so captivated his nascent musical intellect. "But then I decided I was losing my nerve and didn't want to do the song."

When Bentz wrote to the 60s rock star about this reticence, however, McGuinn encouraged him to go for the experience. He wrote that any chance to perform music for fellow human beings was a worthy endeavor. Bentz followed through, sang in public, and a new life began.

Following an appearance as opening act for late Camden blues guitarist Jeff Norwood, Bentz then had the confidence to start performing his own songs, as well as promoting his signature singer-songwriter nights, at clubs like the defunct Red Tub in West Columbia, the old version of the Cock & Bull, and now Utopia. His music career about which he'd dreamed had taken wing.

———

On a breezy April evening, Bentz loads in the P.A. and other musical accoutrements that a one-man music impresario uses to ply his trade. He's his own roadie, his own manager, his own songwriter, his own guitar picker, and this is another night of doing what he loves best: making live music.

On this occasion Bentz Kirby is more, however, than a one-man music road show—yes, it's an otherwise ordinary weekday evening on Rosewood Drive, but inside Utopia it's almost time for Right Bank Rails, which is what Kirby calls the singer-songwriter nights he hosts. Now all he needs is a few courageous, fellow tunesmiths to share the open mic with him.

As he tunes up his "cheap Washburn" guitar, he surveys the early dinner crowd occupying the scattered tables inside and out.

"I hope they're here to check out the music—'cause that's what they're going to get." To Bentz Kirby, music is the bread of life, and sharing that artistic sustenance with like-minded folks is what drives his spiritual and creative life.

Along with the bands and Right Bank Rails, he and his wife May feature house concerts, in which traveling musicians appear in the Kirby living room, playing to small but appreciative audiences. In a town that lacks music venues, he considers these shows, promoted through word of mouth and social media, to be a public service.

Kirby also organizes and promotes annual tributes to past, iconic music festivals like Woodstock and Monterrey Pop, in which local musicians recreate the songbooks of classic rock acts.

His musical energy seems boundless.

Marty Fort, an influential Columbia musician, educator, and booking agent, offers high praise for Kirby: "If every musician in this town cared and promoted as hard as he does, Columbia would be the next Athens or Nashville."

Since October of 2012, however, when all of it nearly came to an end, he's had to slow down. A bit.

While driving home from an upstate family reunion with his wife, Bentz suffered a massive coronary event from which less than one percent who suffer such attacks tend to survive.

Bentz did, though. Somehow.

My theory? The universe isn't finished hearing his songs.

On a more prosaic level, an unlikely series of 'coincidences,' to use a rather spiritually crude and ignorant term, conspired to save his life: an off-duty nurse with a defibrillator in her trunk, an EMT unit, two blocks away, already dispatched and returning from a canceled call. The love and hope of his wife, at his side and praying for his survival.

He went to the other side, albeit only briefly. Came back to report on it to us all.

The first time I saw him after the heart attack, on a visit to his Rosewood area home where he'd been convalescing after the hospital stay, he told me all about his visit to the afterworld, or what seemed that way to him. A tunnel-like event, sure, though it took talking through the memories for him to see his brief journey that way.

"Everyone there was very excited for me, shouting and encouraging me to hurry along, but I felt the love of my wife and family pulling me back. I said, 'I've got to go back. They need me.' And here I am."

He would go on to describe his near-death experience as the most incredibly vivid trips he'd had since his old 60s days of, shall we say, heady experimentation with the sacraments of the interior cosmic voyager. Made this particular writer feel a little less frightened of the end that day, his story of storming the gates of heaven. "Your work here was not done," is the best I could come up with to his tale of there-and-back-again. "You've more songs to sing."

Speaking of those, Kirby's original songs express strong emotions about aging, his family history, and even about the art form itself—his song "Real Music" excoriates the industry machine that cranks out stars rather than artists: You can take your songs that sound the same/pitch corrected singers like Shania Twain/Clear Channel demographics/it's insane.

Another country tune, "Ridin' In My Car," expresses his desire to commune with one of the greats: If I meet Hank Williams' ghost/I hope we can be friends. Other songs reflect a wistfulness for past, youthful road adventures, still others name check more music greats, both famous and otherwise, with whom he has shared experiences.

Besides the above, "Country Music," "Secret World," "Carolina Blues," "Circles," and the autobiographical "Grady County Blues," about a vivid adolescent encounter with both psychedelics and law enforcement, are all titles that will be familiar to listeners of his original work. More than familiar, though, the songs are damn catchy. Listeners may find yourself walking out of the show with an earworm or two. Duly warned.

Bentz might've been slowed down a bit since his medical crisis, but a year later, his recovery has not only progressed, but allowed him to reach a new musical high watermark:

In October 2013, Alien Carnival, having landed a spot opening Georgia's annual Magfest music event, ripped through a set of tunes in the warm autumn sunshine, the biggest showcase yet for Bentz Kirby's songwriting and performing abilities. The gig, which can be heard online at the Internet Archive (Search for 'Alien Carnival Magfest'), is testament to the human spirit, and feels like a minor miracle: that a man who came so close to death—indeed, may have briefly crossed that line—could be capable of such a spirited, joyous performance ought to be inspiring to us all.

One thing's for sure: the inspiration he's provided this writer, on the level of both creativity as well as friendship, makes me glad I finally took that call from 'Vince' all those years ago. My life's been richer for it. In fact, I daresay we've all been blessed here in Columbia, South Carolina, to have Bentz Kirby's songs and friendship to enjoy and appreciate. Long may he sing.

Where the Poet Dwells & the Private Religion of Grief: Ed Madden

By Jennifer Bartell

This is about what happens when a poet becomes a caregiver to a parent dying from cancer. This is about the year 2011 in which two poets lost their fathers. This is about how death, grief, and memory coalesce to find a comfortable residence in lines of poetry. In March 2011 Ed Madden took leave of absence from the University of South Carolina to return to Arkansas to help care for his father, who was dying from pancreatic cancer. He returned home as an unintentional prodigal son. In 2005 I returned home to South Carolina after going to college in Georgia. I returned as a dutiful daughter who wanted to help my father care for my mother.

Two poets become caregivers of ailing parents. Surely there are some similarities in our experiences: chemotherapy, hospice, Jesus. As poets we attempt to find the right words in the right order. But what do we do when the people who gave us life begin slipping from this world? How can we describe this thing that happened and our emotions behind its happening? How do we put thoughts on paper in a way that's clear and somewhat sane, that cuts through the chaos that has invaded our brains?

There is no way for me to completely understand Ed's experience with his father just as there is no way for him to understand my experience with my mother. But empathy is not about the experience: Brené Brown says, "Empathy is connecting with the emotion that someone is experiencing, not the event or the circumstance." The helplessness, the sadness, the hopelessness of not being able to save a loved is emotional. Something that provides a buttress for holding up the hopelessness, for preventing it from being overwhelming, are memories. Ed's chapbook *My Father's House* begins with a poem called "Ark" that describes Ed, as a boy, opening a present during Christmas morning 1966. The Ark is Noah's Ark and the memory unfolds as a child who watches his mother manage a sea of wrapping paper and a father asleep in a reclining chair.

However, "Ark" is not quite that simple. Poetry is the Ark that carried Ed over the flood of emotions that surely must have come with transitioning from a caregiver to the bereaved.

———

Fall semester 2011 was his first one back to USC after his father died. It was my first semester of an MFA in Creative Writing. One week before Fall Break I received a phone call that changed my life. My father had died of a heart attack. Two weeks later I would return to campus carrying with me a purse of grief loaded down with pain. A purse I barely kept from dragging on the ground.

Spring semester 2011 was our first poetry workshop after losing our fathers. He was the professor and I was the student. Grief was still fairly fresh, as it never completely goes stale, and the first book we read was Li-Young Lee's *Rose*, which contains the trope of the dead father. Ed spoke candidly about his father's death and wrote and shared his poems about it with the class. Ed had unknowingly comforted me by making his class about loss and grief. In class, I found a space where I could explore grief through poetry to someone who *understood*. What these books of poetry on grief and loss showed me was that it was possible to use poetry to process grief. They showed me templates for what I could do with grief in my own work. We used poetry as an avenue to process and explore loss and grief.

Public expressions of grief are common during the commemoration of national tragedies such as September 11. Private expressions of mourning are usually reserved for spaces such as the church during a funeral or in the solitude of a home. The *My Father's House* event was the single most important individual expression of grief in public that I have ever seen. The event was a collaboration between composer Paddy Dover and Ed. The show brought together "sound, memory, and image." And provided a place where music, visual art, and poetry could co-exist. In a promotional video for the event, Ed said he had hoped the event showed how a family reconciles watching someone die of cancer and what it does to you when someone you know is dying. He had hoped it resonated for a lot of people. In many families/friendships, there is a lot of silence about these important issues. Although the event was about his individual experience with cancer and grief, the occasion itself created a safe space where a dialogue about cancer, death, and grief was a possibility.

After the event was over, I asked Ed if his family was present. He said they were not. His brother had said he did not want to remember their father "in that way." But isn't that the job of the poet? To dwell in the places people don't want to go. To illuminate what has been shrouded in darkness. The places where the split between grief and life can be sewn back together into a tightly stitched poem. In the poem "Grief" Ed writes, "Grief is a private religion / of color and touch." Ed took this private religion of grief and made it public with the *My Father's House* event. By doing so, he made it bearable. Most people have a family member or a friend or someone they know who has been touched by cancer and/or grief. Often times (where I am from anyway) people don't talk about it openly. It takes residency in the mind, but is seldom verbalized, which means we are unable to empathize (or connect) with one another.

We think of grief as a thing that happens and then ends, but it's more complicated than that, and even more complicated in the life of a poet. This is why it took Tennyson seventeen years to write the long poem *In Memoriam* for his deceased friend. We also read that book in one of the two poetry workshops I'd eventually have with Ed. As poets we reach out into the darkness attempting to solve the riddle of the great weight of death and grief. Poetry works to assuage the riddle. Poetry does not offer *the answer* to the riddle, but it offers *an* approach to answering, a way of looking at it and ultimately a blueprint on how to live with it.

In the movie, *The Shipping News*, Wavey talks to Quoyle about her husband's "death": "It's four years ago and it's today," she says. And this is an appropriate way to describe the phenomenon. It exists on a looping circle that cannot be broken. The immediacy of death, no matter how far away or near it is in time, is felt continuously. Yes, it dissipates over time, but it is always there, beating ceaselessly like waves in an ocean, its presence drifting in and out like the tide.

One memory of sound that sticks with me is listening to my mother breathe on her oxygen machine at night. Later I would attempt to find words to describe those sounds. Words that felt inadequate. However, several years later, I found the way to describe it in one of Ed's poems: "In the dark, the hospice oxygen tank bubbles like an aquarium." It was the perfect words in the perfect order that capture the sound. The next lines are "and in the blue light of their room, my father lies on narrow reef / of bed." The definition of reef is "a ridge of jagged rock, coral, or sand just above or below the surface of the sea." Grief also functions like a reef. It is positioned just above and below the surface of the consciousness. Through his teaching, mentoring, and encouraging of my work, Ed has taught me how to navigate the reef of grief. And that is the lesson I will always treasure the most.

How to Bake the Perfect Loaf of Bread: Marion Mason

By Kara M Gunter

Mason, Marion. Ex-military. Artist. High school art teacher for the past 37 point 5 years. Runs a tight ship in his art classes. Demands excellence and focus. Molds young artists, and doesn't take any gruff. Leave your excuses, and your namby pamby ideas about how anything-is-art-if-you-just-wish-it hard-enough, at the door.

The cool kids just referred to him as Mason. I was shy and awkward, and tried not to speak too high above a whisper, lest anyone actually hear me. I wanted to call him Mason. I couldn't, though, because it was too familiar. So, I called him Mr. Mason, instead.

I tried to go as unnoticed as possible, but I did have "friends". I had a lot of them, in fact, from across the spectrum of social cliques; but interacting with people back then, was like traipsing through a minefield. I was hyper-vigilant, never wanting to appear or sound totally un-cool. Skittering lightly upon the surface of friendships, I never felt truly integrated, and I hung on the fringes of high school society with my notebooks of bad poetry, my sketchbook and my camera. That camera was practically another appendage-- I was on the yearbook staff, after all, saddled with the job of recording the life of the southeastern American teenager. I went to ALL the football games, not because I enjoyed the game, the noise and hysteria, or the hormonally-driven teenage socializing, but because I was required to be there. A total nightmare for a shy introvert, and I approached it all with an internal snarky derision.

It's the only thing that shy, fringy kids have—their sense of scorn. You know you'll never be popular. It's just not in your genes. Popular kids had popular parents, and the status is inherited. They don't want you, anyway. It's not like they take recruits. So, you convince yourself you don't want it, and you convince yourself it's beneath you.

Anyway, this is not a woe-is-me story. I'm just painting a picture for you. A backdrop, perhaps. I've gessoed the canvas, and I'm blocking in my base tones...

The other thing that shy kids have, is that one thing you're really good at, that you've honed. It makes you special, and you wear it like a badge because it's all you got. You're known for that thing. Art was my thing. I'd leave drawings "casually" lying about, and when someone would exclaim, "Dude! That is so cool," I'd shrug and be all like, "What? This doodle? Thanks, man." I mean, it's not like I was getting attention for my academic inclinations. My grades were abhorrent. I was certainly capable, but it was just so boring, and I'd much rather draw, write or daydream than take notes. I once didn't fail a history test based solely on my lyrical knowledge of a Roger Waters song about the history of China.

This is where Mr. Mason comes into the picture, or composition, so to speak. I remember on the first day of art class with Mr. Mason, I tried to impress him by leaving my drawings scattered about my space. The tried and true technique to garner attention, had no effect. He breezed by without looking the least bit impressed. A little wounded, I gathered them up and stuffed them unceremoniously back into my backpack.

This wasn't the last time Mr. Mason would upset my delicate sensibilities. Do you know what he told me-- this child that had been gifted with a gift from the gods themselves? He told me that there was no such thing as talent. Oh, how this turned things on their ear for me! If there was no such thing as talent, then anyone could do what I do. Maybe I'm not so special after all.

Mr. Mason was convinced (and I'm also a convert to this way of thinking) that like anything, art is a skill. It can be taught, and it can be learned. There are a set of rules. There are elements and principles, and there's something called two and three-point perspective that was "discovered" during the Renaissance to help artists draw the illusion of 3-dimensional space on a 2-dimensional surface. He taught me about negative space and how to fill it with positive space. Going right along with my timid demeanor, I drew so lightly on my paper it could hardly be seen. He always made me go back over it, and taught me about varying my drawing pressure.

Art class was not play-time. It was work-time. Art was serious business, and there was a right and wrong way to go about it. There was good art, and there was bad art, and there were real reasons for both that could be discussed and analyzed. Art could be well-made, or badly-made, and it all came down to something called craftsmanship and the level in which the artist employed it. Unintentional smudges, drips, marks, creases, stains = unprofessional, distracting and lazy.

The gift of observation is about the only thing that maybe one is born with. Observation is really the best tool of the most skillful artists. That being said, it can be learned. Mr. Mason taught me to really "see" what was in front of me— to notice the way the light and shadows change, the surface texture, the variety of color found in one small area of any object...

On top of observation, it helps to have a healthy dose of sensitivity, patience, and the ability for objectivity. Those things, sure, they can be taught, but I was born that way. So, maybe I am a little bit special. All those moments standing on the edge of the hub-bub of the quintessential teenage existence, pointing my camera into the fray, squinting through the viewfinder, waiting for the perfect moment, holding my breath, then—SNAP!—capturing the perfect moment, memorializing it in thousands of yearbooks. My point of view is forever there. Anyone can see what life looks like from the edges, now.

Mr. Mason took something I dabbled in and challenged me to take it to the next level. He pushed me constantly, and helped me develop my conceptual ideas. Taking an independent study-based art class from him, he'd look through my sketchbooks, and read my notes and offer suggestions, dodge-and-burn (to use darkroom vernacular) my ideas to perfect them. He didn't shy away from the teenage angst and dissatisfaction. Mr. Mason, in a really subtle way I never noticed until I was an adult, helped me spit-polish those ideas and sophisticate them. Morose and disquiet drawings, gave way to the conceptual and experimental experiences in the darkroom. I began layering portraits of friends, under transparencies of my written poetry, and double exposures.

Earlier in the year, we'd read an article about how the National Endowment of the Arts was in danger of losing its funding with critics siting examples like Mapplethorpe's entire body of work, and Serrano's controversial Piss Christ. Mr. Mason assigned a paper on the subject, and we had a class discussion or two around the topic. To this day, I have no idea of what Mr. Mason's opinion was on the whole thing. He was that good of a teacher that he kept his own opinion out of it, while encouraging us each to think critically, and form our own opinions. Each view point, as it arose and if expressed intelligently, was given equal weight.

At some point, I'd decided that I wanted to make my own interpretation of Piss Christ, exploring the humanity of the Christ figure—an aspect of the Christ I felt was too often ignored. I had this idea to dress one of my friends (a preacher's son, no less) as Jesus and photograph him from behind, standing in front of a urinal. I was worried Mr. Mason would talk me out of it. I wasn't trying to be offensive, or even particularly shocking, though I was hoping to strike a nerve, and make a point. Frankly, the idea of being offensive scared me. As you know by now, I wasn't comfortable being noticed.

Some were going to be offended by the portrait, that's just the way it was. Some people were going to fail to get the point, and even if they did, they may still disagree. But Mr. Mason encouraged me to express myself, and made the classroom a safe place for the young mind to grow, expand, ask questions, doubt itself, celebrate itself, and be itself. I made the portrait. And even all these years later, I still consider it one of the first glimpses I have of my artist's self and one of the first peeps of my artist's voice.

I'm writing a lot about the development of myself as an artist. But really, it's bigger than that. That time was about my development as a human. If I were a loaf of bread—stay with me—then what Mr. Mason did, was add some leaveners to my pasty, stringy self. By the time I'd left high school, I'd risen to doughy ball of goodness, and I was ready to go into the oven and do my bready thing. I could have been flat, unleavened, and perhaps a little boring, but instead, now I'm all set to make a fine loaf of brioche. I'm still baking, but I'll let you know how I turn out.

I'm a teacher now, and believe me, it's the last place I thought I'd end up. The crippling shyness hung around until my mid-20's, and I would have literally died if you'd told me I'd be talking freely, and expressing myself in front of a classroom full of students.

I think about Mr. Mason's classes constantly. WWMMD? What would Mr. Mason do? Not to be self-deprecating, but I don't think I'm nearly as good of a teacher as Mr. Mason is. I do think I'm pretty good, and I'm sure I'll get better with experience, but the high bar I've set for myself was actually set by Mr. Mason.

I channel him when I scold students for bringing up the dreaded "T" word (talent). I forcefully, and with no apologies, tell them to dismiss that drivel. I try my best, in a semester, to deprogram the wrong-headed, feel-good idea that art is anything you want it to be. Don't make me barf with that saccharine B.S.! Art is work. It's hard, and it should be. It takes time and practice, dedication and discipline. There are rules, and when one has become well-versed in those rules, only then may one think of breaking them with audacity and purpose. Art is not a hobby. It's a job. Show up, stop whining and get to work. That's what makes you special—not your so-called talent. It's your dedication to the endeavor that sets you apart.

Recently, Mason told me I could call him Marion. I just can't. I'm almost 40, and I can't bring myself to call my revered art teacher by his first name. I have, however, graduated to the simple and familiar "Mason". I feel like I've earned my chops. I'm a late bloomer, and it took a long while, but I'm finally one of the cool kids. I still abhor football, and that's a difficult stance to have in the South, but at least I do not exist quietly on the fringes anymore. I'm in the fray of it, and thanks to Mason, I'm a half-baked loaf of lovely brioche.

Superhero: Darion McCloud

By Jon Tuttle

It's a simple question: "What is it you *do*?"

Actually, it's a ridiculous question. Everyone knows Darion McCloud, everyone knows what he does, and everyone has a favorite Darion McCloud story. When he joins me for coffee this morning, everyone in the joint turns to look. He's that kind of guy: big, imposing, electric, magnetic. Those who come over to say hello are greeted with his wide smile and a bear hug. He's *that* kind of guy.

He's renowned in the Midlands as a storyteller, educator and arts activist. For years he's been a constant presence on Columbia stages in such roles as Walter Lee in *A Raisin in the Sun*, Clay in *Dutchman* or Lincoln in *Topdog/Underdog*. With Trustus, with Theatre USC, with Workshop Theatre or with the South Carolina Shakespeare Company, Darion has acted in or directed some the best plays of the American stage.

And of course with NiA, his production company. Now a familiar institution in its own right, NiA was founded in 1998 as an extension of Trustus Theatre's African-American Acting Workshop. Its original goal was pretty straight-forward: to create acting opportunities for black actors seeking to control their own artistic lives. Soon, however, he and NiA found a wider purpose: to "tell stories other people won't tell," stories for and about local audiences, all for a low admission price.

So okay, everyone knows all that. This morning I'll discover that Darion is also a visual artist—that he finished a degree in studio arts from the University of South Carolina and has had solo shows at the Atlanta Arts Festival, the Koger Center and Benedict College, and that for a while he worked at the Columbia Museum of Art as an outreach manager.

And that he's a model. That's a watercolor Darion on the cover and throughout *Dave The Potter: Artist, Poet, Slave* (Little, Brown 2010), an illustrated history of the Edgefield slave who inscribed his remarkable pottery with his own verse. Darion also portrayed Dave in a documentary film, *Discovering Dave: Spirit Captured in Clay,* produced in 2013 by the South Carolina Institute of Archaeology and Anthropology.

He does so many things, really, that he should be wearing a bright red cape. But if he had a business card, what would it say?

He thinks about that. "I call myself an artist," he says, sort of sheepishly. "But I don't have a real elevator speech."

I've known Darion for years, at least since 2001, when he and the late and legendary Greg Leevy helped me create *The White Problem,* a play about the first black professor at the University of South Carolina. The text demanded that Darion play about ten different characters, including W.E.B. DuBois, Booker T. Washington and a white redneck agitator, morphing from one to the next with but a gesture, a posture, an accent. That's when I learned what a workhorse he is: always where he's supposed to be, always thinking/asking/deciding, always brimming with optimism and an infectious energy. The show rehearsed for a month, opened at USC's Longstreet Theatre, then travelled to Piccolo Spoleto and a few area universities. It was a great experience, a great group, but then it ended, and we all went back to our real lives.

Which is why I wanted to write about him. For as long as I've known him, I've wondered what Darion's real life is. You know: the thing he does, how he pays his rent. I can't imagine that any of his projects, by itself, provides a steady income. Few have shelf lives longer than a few weeks. Anyone who pursues a career in the arts learns very early that it will likely have to be subsidized by a day job, and Darion knows he is no exception. He admits that keeping NiA going for sixteen years has been "crazy hard," primarily because it's nomadic, sometimes rehearsing in five different spaces in a single week. Of his personal finances, he concedes that "being poor—well, not rich—it affects your self-worth."

So here's the real question, then: *why*? Why would a now middle-aged man with so many marketable skills commit himself so completely to perpetrating art when the benefits package is so dubious?

His answer will come much later in the conversation, once he's sifted through the layers of memory, connected the dots in his life, and arrived at his daughter. When he talks about her his face will change. He'll tip his head a little to the right, and his eyes will soften, and he'll say this: "I just think art can make everything better. I try to make things better using art." For a moment or two he'll ponder that, then add, "Good art is good *for* you. That's what I've based my life on."

But first we go back. In no particular order, according to no chronology, he recounts the turning points he didn't know were turning points, like the time somebody saw him telling stories at Richland County Library and gave his name to Jocelyn Sanders at Trustus. She summoned him to a cattle-call audition for the *The Salvation of Iggy Scrooge*, a Christmas rock-opera directed by Tim Gardner. Darion had no idea what to expect. At the time, he was "starving as an artist" so the prospect of acting "made me giddy and shit."

He was cast, almost on-sight, as the Ghost of Bob Marley. Gardner remembers the night well: "We were wrapping up a long, disappointing casting day when in swaggers this mountain of a man with dreadlocks and a movie star smile. I remember mumbling to myself, 'Dear God, please be good. Please be my Bob Marley.' He wasn't good—he was *great*. Darion radiated confidence though he had no formal theatre experience. He asked for direction, then took it and ran with it. Through the rehearsal period I grew to admire and love him for being a wonderful human being. He was the real deal, and on opening night the crowd was buzzing with, 'Where the hell did *this* guy come from?'"

Good question. Darion's answer: "My life had kind of prepared me for the stage." That preparation began at his childhood home on College Place, in the poverty-stricken, sometimes crime-ridden Eau Clare neighborhood. Fortunately, his mother, Bessie, now 73, ran a tight ship, raising her five children by herself. Darion describes her fondly as "a real marshmallow" and then even more fondly as "a real hard-ass. I mean old school. She didn't take a lot of shit."

From her and his surroundings, he learned two things. The first was selflessness. "The thing was: if you can help people, you help people. I was a post-civil rights era kid. Even in my neighborhood there were people modeling for me—just taking care of people, taking care of kids. People were always giving to me. It makes you realize how many people are looking out for you."

And so he and his family gave back. "We grew up in the Kool Aid house," he smiles. He talks about his siblings, Marcus, Laryssa, Trevor and Lavette—now deceased—and describes his childhood home as a great hive of activity. "There were always kids around. There were great families. I look back now and I realize how cool and unique that was. We thought of ourselves as family. We still do."

The other lesson was versatility, the instinct to survive by fitting in, getting along, reading the terrain. "I was a library nerd," he recalls. "I was the nerd kid, I was the jock kid, I was a wanna-be thug-kid, a stoner kid, and I was in classes with the smart kids. I got a good education on how to navigate all these groups of people." And this, he suspects, fed his instincts as an actor.

So did football, which he played (on scholarship) for Fort Valley State University in Georgia, and then, albeit briefly, at the University of South Carolina. "Being an athlete," he recalls, "I was used to being judged. I was used to being *abused*. So that first time I hit the stage, it felt fuckin' right. I respected the people there, their discipline, even their physical toughness."

Respect. Discipline. Toughness. He says such things and I am reminded of his performance as Levee in *Ma Rainey's Black Bottom* at Trustus in 2003. I recall his bluster, his power, his angry knife-fight with God. I recall such things and I cannot believe this is the same Darion McCloud who devotes so much of his time and talent to entertaining other people's children.

Which is actually why I wanted to write about him. This is a man who brings the same level of commitment to *Rumplestiltskin* and *Br'er Rabbit* as he did to *Othello*. This is the "mountain of a man" behind such kid-friendly fare as *Holla* and *Whatchamacallit*. This is the man Heather Leigh, Nia's company manager, calls "everybody's big brother."

"I think what makes him so remarkable," says Leigh, "is that he doesn't just want to be transformed by art. He wants his art to transform his community. That's how much he cares about people, and he cares for them deeply, no matter who they are. I've seen him walk into a room and walk out with new friends and I *do* mean friends."

Working with kids, of course, is not just thankless—it's treacherous. They get bored quickly and are quick to tell you about it, and they can tell when they're getting preached to. "Kids can spot a phony," says Jim Thigpen, founding artistic director at Trustus. "But they're putty in Darion's hands. He understands that good acting is, after all, good story telling. He has spent many years working hard to bring the arts to those who have been historically ignored by the arts community. Bottom line, he is a genuine and genuinely-talented good guy."

Kate Fox, executive director at Harbison Theatre, concurs. "Darion intends for everyone to be involved in each creative moment," she says, "whether as performer, designer, or spectator, and to learn and be changed. He exhibits a mastery of his craft but an unwillingness to be stagnant in his pursuit of excellence. He has a great laugh, a strong intellect, and a wide heart. There aren't many people I admire more than Darion."

"Or Michaela, for that matter," Fox adds, meaning Darion's partner, sculptor and performance artist Michaela Brown, whom he met at the Columbia Museum of Art. Together they're collaborating on what Darion calls "the best thing I've ever done in my life."

Her name is Zaire, and she's six.

When he speaks of her, he is clearly thinking of his own childhood, of the many mentors who made a difference for him. "Now I have a person in my home that *I'm* responsible for," he says. "I have to feed her brain, her body, her soul." He tells the story of a tantrum she once threw in a store, when he wouldn't buy her a doll she wanted. "I told her, 'we're going to go buy stuff for babies who don't have anything.'" So together they went around selecting clothes for needy children, "and she got the fever."

He talks like a rich guy. "I think about legacy with her," he says, and he tips his head a little to the right. "It's all about legacy. I want people to say, 'he raised a good daughter—he raised a good *woman*.' I need her to be strong so when the world comes at her she can still get out the door."

Which is why there is now Story Squad, an ensemble of costumed crusaders with names like Blossom, Drum Machine Mr. One and Two, and Guitar Warrior—all Columbia-area artists who "sing stories and tell songs, travelling the universe and making it safe for kids." Darion created Story Squad in 2012, when Fox approached him about creating a series for families and children with learning disabilities. It has since performed around the Midlands and surrounding areas and has been snowballing of late. Darion foresees tee-shirts, activity books and, he hopes, sponsorships. On its Facebook page is a cover shot of Squadron member Bonita "Mother

Nature" Peeples, wearing what appears to be a flower arrangement shower cap and belting out a big ol' song with The Captain—Darion, in dark blue coveralls, flight goggles...

...and a bright red cape.

Which brings me to my favorite Darion McCloud story. Reggie Harvey, area actor and longtime NiA member, tells it. A parent had brought her son to the children's room at Richland County Library to hear Darion tell stories. Now she was back, wanting to find him and ask if she could borrow one of his hats.

"Her child had decided," says Reggie, "that for Halloween, he wanted to be Mr. Darion.

"Not Superman, Batman, Spiderman or Ironman"

"Not Optimus Prime, Harry Potter, or a light saber-wielding Jedi Knight."

"He wanted to go trick-or-treating as Mr. Darion."

"Darion McCloud is a superhero"

Remembering: Carrie McCray

By Randy Spencer

"Living memory holds the dead as a hand holds water. . ."
—*Jane Hirshfield writing of her friend, poet Czclaw Milosz, after his death*

It was emotionally difficult to write this. I knew Carrie for the last twenty years of her life, almost from the time she came to live in Columbia. The Carrie I knew was not so much the public figure, the poet showered with honors, but a private Carrie, soft-spoken, modest, someone who welcomed me into the home she shared with her sister, Rose, and their dog. Someone who came when I cooked out in my backyard, who sat around my kitchen table planning a Writers' Workshop conference. Someone I picked up at night when she could no longer drive after dark, and drove her to a reading we both had in a bookstore, a setting where Carrie's voice was no match for the latte machine whirring nearby.

Her illness, her death startled me. She had seemed ageless, both young at heart and old in the sense of having wisdom bought with long experience. If anything, I have two last memories. The first: in October 2007, nine months before her death, was at the Columbia Museum of Art. I had gone to see and hear Carrie's poems, a last book re-telling the tragic story of Ota Benga, transformed into a celebration of words, music, and dance. When the performance ended I went down to speak to her and Carrie bent down from the stage and kissed me on the forehead. A grandmotherly kiss, which was the way I thought of her. An affectionate, caring grandmother-in-poetry, always listening, always encouraging.

The second memory is more sobering: nine months later, when Carrie had suffered a stroke and had been admitted to a aftercare facility in West Columbia, I went to the nurses' desk and asked her room number by her name, "Carrie McCray," and was told she wasn't there. She wasn't. In the nine months since I had seen her, Carrie had remarried, this time to John Nickens, a friend for eighty years. I found Carrie Allen McCray Nickens alone, unresponsive, at least in any obvious way. I sat by her bed, touched her hand, and read her own poems to her from The South Carolina Collection, where we had both been published. They were poems of memory, of grief, of her own resilience. There was a poem taken from her childhood:

> . . . my mother
> with silken cover
> takes my hand and
> thick, tangled hair
> to the Poro lady
> a long day in the hot-comb
> hair-greased rooms
> . . . I return home
> with curls. . .

I had needed to ask what a Poro lady was. But another from that first published selection painted a dark hint at the backstory of her family that came out later. In "Nobody Wrote a Poem," she wrote of herself growing up:

Nobody wrote a poem
about me
In ugly tones they
Called me "Yaller Gal"
How lovely to have been
born black or brown
Pure substance the artist
could put his pen to
Not something in between—
diluted, undefined, unspecific
I search the poets
for words of me. . .
yet I'm not sure. . .
"caramel treats". . ."brown sugars". . .
"plum tinted blacks". . .
I, born out of history's
Cruel circumstance. . .
and nobody wrote a poem

This second poem can only be understood knowing the back story of Carrie's family, her white grandfather in her later memoir, *Freedom's Child: The Life of a Confederate General's Black Daughter*. Almost always when something is written about Carrie, the piece will begin with a quote or paraphrase from the first page of her book about her mother: She begins with her own memory:

"When we were very young, we lived in a big yellow house across the road from the campus of Virginia Seminary in Lynchburg, Virginia. In Mama's bedroom there was a huge four-antique bed, the "birthing bed" where all except one of her ten children were born. In that same room, on the mantelpiece above the fireplace, was a picture of a white man in uniform. I don't ever remember asking who he was. In later years my brother Hunter told me it was a picture of Mama's father, a Confederate general named Jones. . . . Mama never talked about her father. . . . Years ago nobody talked about things like that. . ."

There is another story a few pages later where Carrie describes the wife of her grandfather, saying that she must have been a kind and genteel woman, that even after her mother and uncle were born, her grandmother continued to work in the General's home. The story tells how:

"Once General's wife asked Malinda to bring Mary to see her, which she did. Before they left, General's wife gave Mary a porcelain-headed doll that had belonged to Mrs. Jones when she was a child. . . . when Mary thanked Mrs. Jones and hugged her, Mrs. Jones reached over and kissed her on the forehead. . . . Mary visited her often before Mrs. Jones died." The General's wife had been ill for some time; she had never had a child of her own. The General, Carrie relates, always recognized Malinda and her brother as his own, and was ostracized for doing so.

When I first knew Carrie we met as a small group in the meeting room of a past-its-prime motel on Bush River Road to workshop each other's writing, but went on to envision the creation of the South Carolina Writers Workshop. Carrie rightfully gives credit in the Acknowledgments in *Freedom's Child* to Scott Regan as the driving force, although we were all on the Board. From the early days of the Workshop came several years of somewhat grandiose gatherings of eager would-be and accomplished writers at meetings, at first on the coast, then in Columbia. Carrie brought her friend,

Toi Derrocotte, to lead one session. Although the rest of us were always worried about budgets and money and how we could cover the cost of such elaborate undertakings, Scott never seemed concerned. The organization survived and continues to survive with an annual recognition of Carrie with an award in her name. But from the growing membership came the South Carolina Collection in 1991, the volume from which I read to Carrie when I last saw her, where we both published small selections of poetry.

Carrie's modesty, and her sense of privacy, was such that none of us realized for a long while the full story she would tell of her family. When she first started to discuss it, she wanted their lives to be portrayed as fiction—a novel—and we urged her to go forward as memoir instead. *Freedom's Child* is primarily about her mother, and the story was built on library research and long interviews with people who had known her, but Carrie is part of the story, too. She was the ninth of ten children and was in her early twenties when her mother died. Older siblings helped piece together the picture of a woman who was a pioneer in the fight for equal rights for Black children, pushing the schools in New Jersey to open up extra-curricular opportunities—even graduation ceremonies—to all students. She fought against the church's resistance to Black girls dancing, bringing evidence from the Bible of dancing in times of joy.

There was a relatively brief 3 years where Carrie's childhood overlapped the last years before Ota Benga's death, but his life provided the basis for the poetry in her last book. Ota's history was covered first in *Freedom's Child* where he was called Otto, the name her brothers used for him. Ota died on March 20, 1916. He had hidden a gun in the hay inside an old shed and shot himself. His suicide in his mid-thirties ended a life that traveled from the Congo to America. Ota was a pigmy, four feet nine inches tall, and he had been stolen from his family—his wife and children—first, to be exhibited with other aboriginal peoples from different parts of the world in the St. Louis World's Fair in 1904 as an examples of the lower species of man. Later he was put on display as part of an exhibit in the Bronx Zoo, in a cage with monkeys. He was rescued through the protests and threats by Black ministers, and came to live with Carrie's mother's first husband as his guardian at Virginia Seminary in Lynchburg, Virginia. When Professor Hayes died, Ota was placed back in an orphanage in Brooklyn.

In 1910 he was given his wish to return to Carrie's mother's home. She re-married, this time to Carrie's father, and at the time Carrie was born in 1913 Ota had been accepted almost like a sibling by her brothers. But however much he seemed to enjoy living there at first, he grew more and more homesick for Africa, and even though his return to his family had been promised, there was no money to pay his passage back. On the afternoon before his death, he gathered wood and built a fire in a field near the house. Several of Carrie's brothers watched as he danced feverishly around the fire, faster and faster, making "strange sounds as he danced, chanting, moaning." That was the last time anyone saw Ota alive.

Carrie's moving tribute to Ota Benga was finally published four years after her death, five years after she saw it performed on stage with the musical and vocal score by her close friend, Kevin Simmonds. In the poetry she wrote, sometimes in the voice of Ota himself, as when he was in the zoo:

> "I'm like a wind, go and come, go
> and come, sometime soft
> like a breeze, sometime bad like
> a storm. . . .
>
> I don't know where I am."

Or at Carrie's home:

> "I fall asleep
> in woods, dream of antelope, smell fire of
> home. Call *Kemba, Kemba time for
> hunt*. Take off running. . . ."

Or:

> "I'm a forest man
> where me and the wind like brother
> . . .
> I belong in forest
> I belong in forest
> I belong in forest

The poems chant and moan, call out Ota's tragic story, unforgettable as Carrie's voice as though it had never gone away.

There are postscripts to the chronicle of our relationship. Carrie's funeral overflowed with people who had loved and admired her, but I remember more the next year when she was inducted into the South Carolina Academy of Authors with some of her surviving family present. Lastly, in 2012, I had a role in the introducing *Ota Benga Under My Mother's Roof* at the South Carolina Book Festival. That was the last time I saw her sister, Rosemary.

I suspect there may have been another episode in my own life, interest in which was heightened by Carrie's memoir and poetry. I began searching for the history of my great-grandfather. He was an enlisted man and had fought for the South, most noticeably at the Battle of the Crater near Petersburg, Virginia. He survived, as did his five brothers who fought alongside him. After the war he became a minister and served in churches from Virginia to South Carolina. The ruins of one church where he preached can be found today near Darlington. But I visited the still-standing home where he was born, a single large room, unsafe now to walk inside, with a loft, where fourteen children were born, seven to each of two mothers. Behind the ramshackle home, hidden in the underbrush and covered in vines, were the remains of a slave cabin. If Carrie has lasting effects on the people she knew, one way is to prompt them to tell their own stories, our personal histories, however private, however painful, with candor and honestly that will resonate with readers.

"It is very difficult to live with silence."

A Love Letter: Ray McManus

By Susan Levi Wallach

In other circumstances, this might be a love letter. The first time I saw Ray McManus—in a hall of Columbia's Richland Northeast High School—I thought, That's one hot dude. What does he teach? At the time, I handled RNE's press and public relations and always needed a compelling media pitch. Here stood a likely prospect. I found out he taught in the Palmetto School of the Arts Literary Arts magnet. Though the literary arts program at RNE is long dead, Ray thrives, writing poetry that can wring your heart or make you squirm or get you thinking of all the sorrows and miracles in this world.

I wound up writing the first article about Ray—a press release, really, but it ran in a number of local weeklies. It was 2004. At that point, he had three published poems on his CV, all in small literary journals. He was finishing his MFA at the University of South Carolina, working with, among others, Ed Madden, who was his thesis adviser, and Kwame Dawes. But in the PCA magnet, Ray was a star, the guy who made kids want to explore metaphor, to reveal their hidden selves in short line bursts, to respond to writing prompts, to read and discuss each other's work as if it were the latest video game and they'd discovered all the cheats. He brought USC's Split P poetry outreach program to the RNE campus, and suddenly kids from throughout the school district were giving up their Sunday afternoons to write and talk about poetry. It was something magnificent to see: true education, in the sense of illuminating and elucidating and inspiring. The world made both clear and mysterious all at once. My son was one of his students; I kept his notebook from that year, and it isn't the poetry that astonishes me but the determination he put into draft after draft the perseverance to come up with his best work. That's a life lesson in itself.

At that time, Ray seemed to be among the world's least likely poets, a man whose early life groomed him for something else: motorcycle mechanic, trucker, house painter. Honest-day's-work professions—and maybe a few others that were not so honest—none involved with meter or metaphor or enjambment or Ray's particular way of phrasing.

In the head-up-its-ass teach-for-the-test world of public K-12 education, an artist without teaching credentials is an artist without a job. It's a shame, because ten years later, there is no literary arts program at RNE—no Split P or South Carolina Poetry Initiative, for that matter—but Ray is thriving. He has his doctorate, an assistant professorship at USC Sumter, and, most important, two published books of poetry (*Driving Through the Country in which You Were Born* and *Red Dirt Jesus*) with a third (*Punch*) scheduled for release in fall 2014. *Driving Through the Country in which You Were Born* won the South Carolina Poetry Book Prize. *Red Dirt Jesus* won the first Marick Press Poetry Prize. *Punch* has already won my heart, my admiration, and, as uncool as it is to admit, my envy. Oh, man—what I would give to write like that: to be able to take the most unremarkable of experiences and turn it into something not only magical and compelling but universal.

When you hear Ray read you hear a voice confident in its meters and rhythms. You don't hear the boy who grew up working class and struggled academically until he found a subject that knocked him off the straight line to nowhere, yanked at his soul, and coalesced his life. The subject, of course, was poetry. Not that the teenage Ray wandered into a library and thought to check out a book of rhymes. Take a look at his "Freshman" from his upcoming collection *Punch* to get a sense of Ray adolescent and fists in a ball:

> Lunch detention meant trash
>
> pickup. There was a drainage
>
> ditch behind the swing sets
>
> and a zipper was stuck, so she
>
> had to work hard to free it.

One day, he landed in the library for yet another school infraction—the teacher said he was smoking; he now says, "I wasn't at that particular time." The librarian, at a loss for what to do with this punk, decided to keep him occupied (or up the punishment) with a poetry anthology titled "Sound and Sense." In ten minutes, Ray's life changed.

"It was about the music of poetry and had really cool poems not in textbook," he remembers. "I was looking at language and words I'd never heard before. I wanted to write song lyrics. I wanted to write things that would blow girls away." He still has the book.

He still has that edge, too, but it's not so much the punk strut anymore. That's pretty much gone, superseded by fatherhood and middle age. But there still is nothing tweedy about Ray. He has the scruffy beard, yes, but also broad shoulders and well-developed biceps—from his years of working for a tree service, he says, which he did "till it was no longer cool to walk into a class at USC smelling of pine sap and sweat. I liked having the money, but I blew it all on pot and girls and gas." Then there are the tats, maybe thirty-two hours' worth of ink.

Ray reads his poems the way a good storyteller spins a tale. No matter where the podium is—on a stage, in an acoustical nightmare of a gallery, in a cavernous atrium—he creates an intimacy with the audience, a one-to-oneness. He builds a narrative, weaving his poems into whole cloth with the stories behind them or just with stories.

As it did in 2004, his professional life follows three strands: teacher and academic, yes, but poet most of all. And what he said then in our first interview still holds true for him:

"What I found in poetry is a conduit. A lot of times when you're writing poetry you're looking around and seeing relationships that you might not otherwise see. These are relationships that most people might never put together. That's the whole magic of metaphor—a wonderful learning apparatus. We're able to compare things we know to things that we don't know but can learn through those comparisons. It becomes a natural education process. They start making those connections in math class, in science. We get students to become more actively engaged in that thought process."

Back then, he would lope into RNE at midday for his afternoon creative-writing classes or, during the summer, for his Tri-DAC workshops. He'd be smiling, relaxed, happy to be in those halls in a purposeful way, and I'm sure that the irony of being a teacher in a competitive magnet program wasn't lost on him: way back when, Ray didn't qualify for a traditional academic diploma—he got a GED, then enrolled at Midlands Tech before moving on to USC for his BA, MFA, PhD, and, currently, a faculty position at USC Sumter (bet that librarian would be surprised).

No matter what the age group, he takes the words "actively engage" seriously, interacting with his students as if they are already writers with the ability to take control of the language and move it in various, deliberate directions. And so they become those writers. In his RNE days, if I needed a photograph of rapt students I went to Ray's class to take it. If I needed a boost for my own writing, I sat in for a while. The syllabus he handed out in my son's year had more in common with a graduate-level poetry workshop than with the typical high school course: "We will write poetry, read and discuss work by contemporary poets—since good writers are inevitably good readers—and hone our critical-thinking skills by critiquing the drafts created in our class. . . . If you consider a poem finished, complete, or highly personal, do not turn it in. This is a workshop; we are here to help each other write more effectively, not admire without comment." He emphasized the importance of making every word count, the fallacy of thinking that creativity is something that just happens and shouldn't be messed with.

Creativity turned out to be his savior. Growing up, he says, "I didn't have time to dream or think about other possibilities. When I finally got settled in school and realized that you can do that kind of stuff, it turned me on. Poetry is an art form that makes you human. Science and math don't teach you to have a compassionate response to the world around you."

I learned about courage from Ray, about owning up to your history without whining about it. It takes pluck to mine some of the areas Ray digs into, if for no other reason that they lack an innate poeticism. Read the first stanza of "Saturday Mornings":

> To break the rabbit, hold
>
> it by its back legs and whip it
>
> forward. My neighbor has
>
> names for his. He tells me
>
> it's a myth that rabbits scream,
>
> but I don't believe him,
>
> and he yawns as he tosses
>
> a wet clump of fur on the table.

That initial image catches you unaware. It is startling in its precision and dispassion, which is then sustained: a good deal of the poem's effect lies in the neighbor's naming of the animal before he uses his hands to kill it and in his nonchalant yawn before tossing the bloodied body on the table, as if he does his killing in the kitchen. It also comes from the weight of the narrator's "I don't believe him." This is a dystopian pastoral for sure.

Ray can invoke a despair in his writing that is hard to reconcile with his demeanor. But for that librarian, he might have grown into a different person, maybe the one in "Minimum Wage" or "How to Add a Porch to a Trailer." In his writing he repeatedly revisits his working-class, somewhat-hardscrabble roots, as if still trying to find the through line from that life to this. I sometimes wonder if in his manual-labor/rough-living poems he is drawing a parallel with his current writerly academic existence: both have their contemplative elements, their down-and-dirty work, though in poetry the heavy lifting lies in the stillness of revision, revision, revision. The trick for the poet is to make the final product (is there ever a final product?) feel effortless, unforced, like it all remarkably just came to mind.

It may just come to mind, but it's never effortless. Beyond inspiration and a facility with words, a poet needs energy and focus and time. And, almost always, a job around which the writing needs to fit. Ray also has a family: his wife is Lindsay Green, a teacher and poet, and he has three children from his two marriages. As he once put it, "I'd love to sit and write every morning till eleven, but. . . ." But . . . like most writers, he's writing even when he isn't. "A poet's job, first of all, is to be an observer, to be a witness and be mindful of that," he says. "For a serious poet, it is both a blessing and a curse. For most part, I am composing in my head. Sometimes the lines haunt me, force me to write them. That's what I meant about the curse of being the observer You can't let anything go. I haven't gone to an event—a birthday party, a wedding—in the last ten, twelve years without constantly thinking, Is there a poem there?

The joy comes when the poem is done, when it is published, when a book is published, when he does a reading. "But the creation is work, even if it's work you love," he says. "At two in the morning when you go to finally crash and this line hits you and you know theres's no way you'll remember it in the morning, you have to get up and write. Or when you see the mountain of student papers you need to grade and you can't focus on them because you're wrestling with last line of this poem that's been haunting you for days. There's no real joy in that. The goal that you tell yourself is there is what propels you. I think the reason that some writers eventually blow their brains out is because that joy of finishing is not there anymore, for whatever reason.

There are certain people whose good opinion matters more than the rest. In my life, Ray is one of those people. A touchstone. Someone whose work I turn to for inspiration, because I know that whatever rut I'm in, it can get me out, give me a sense of a world far larger than my petty distractions and concerns. Ray—his writing—gets me back on track and gives me something to strive for: that metrical truth-or-dare that drives his poems forward, that makes you wish his experiences were yours at the same time that you thank God they aren't—because in your hands they wouldn't be poetry but the end of poetry. Existence without a point, without reflection, and you can see yourself in that kind of life and it is terrifying.

As for the love letter, that's for another lifetime, another world. Or maybe it's what this all turned out to be.

The Drama of Writing:
Cassie Premo Steele

By Brandi L. Perry

"the beginning lies in poetry, for poetry provides distinctive access to pain."

--Cassie Premo Steele

I'm days away from my deadline. Too close for comfort. I've spent the last few weeks thinking about how to condense and articulate my relationship with Cassie – one of the most influential of my writing career – in an essay. Nonfiction, after all, is shorthand for the art of distillation.

Do I begin with the day we met? It was in December 2012 at a benefit for Sexual Trauma Services of the Midlands at Conundrum Music Hall. We were both there to read poetry and raise awareness about sexual assault. I only knew her through her work; specifically, through reading her poetry collection, *The Pomegranate Papers,* for a review in *Jasper* magazine. The review was positive, save for my concern that birthing was so heavily equated with womanhood. I imagined my sister reading the book, my sister who cannot have children, and being devastated. Later, after months of working with Cassie in workshops and coaching sessions, after she taught me to write in a way that was caring and compassionate, after she was the midwife to my first book, I learned that birthing is so much more than physical. Yes, women birth children, but we also birth stories, dreams, and seeds of ideas planted last season that have only now started to blossom.

It was frightening to meet her, as I was worried that she'd been offended by my review. Instead, she smiled at me, resonating a warmth and glow that I would find out was the essential her; whenever I see her, she always radiates positive energy. Thinking back, I'm sure it was the smile of a wise woman looking upon one who has just started down her path.

Beginnings are hard. As a writer, I always think there will be a time when they become easy, when putting words on the page is simpler – to the point where I wake up with words spilling out of me, I'd just have to catch them. Though some days are like this, it is rare. More often, I sit in my downtown apartment, staring at the blank page. Today is one of those days. Instead of waking up and going to my desk, I wake with a feeling of resentment and failure held over from the night before.

Saturday was the fourth anniversary of the death of my boyfriend Bryan's mother. MaryJo Anne Tupper was fifty-seven when she passed of lung cancer that metastasized to her brain. Understanding Bryan's grief is impossible for me. It is a gulf between us – one of the few ways I feel totally disconnected from him. Both of my parents are still alive, and I've never had anyone close to me die. I tried to make the day about him, about distraction and forging new, happier memories by volunteering to dance with my belly dance troupe from Alegria Dance Studio at the Eau Claire Fest. It seemed the perfect way to bring a scrap of joy into his day.

That morning, I planned to get flowers and a card for him. Instead, we cleaned the apartment frantically after one of my belly buddies messaged to say she was coming over to get ready. I made the offer the day before, but no one responded. I assumed no one was coming, so we didn't clean the apartment. Already, unwittingly, the day became about me and it continued to be about me – getting my costuming packed and in the car, getting me drinks on the way so I wouldn't get heatstroke, and just getting me there on time. It because worse after I stepped on a piece of glass onstage and had to hobble back to the car. Bryan had me get in the car and took care of packing my large suitcase and cooler in the backseat.

We went to the Cracker Barrel off of Bush River Road for a dinner of biscuits and gravy - one of his mother's favorite dishes. I was so exhausted from the ninety-degree heat, and then frozen by the too-high air conditioning in the restaurant, that I didn't even think about picking up the check. Later, as we sat in bed eating icecream that I got us from Sonic, he said how much he did for me during the day and how little I did for him. He didn't want to say it, but it had been building up through the course of the day. He didn't understand that I danced for him, was vulnerable on stage for him. That the whole reason I volunteered was for him. I hadn't articulated this, so he didn't know. I had failed. I cried myself to sleep thinking of how I had ruined everything and how selfish I was.

In the morning, when I again plan to write, I leave the house after telling Bryan that I have an errand to run. I'm not warm to him. In all honesty, I'm still hurt by his words and disappointed in myself. I didn't know how to act the day before. He couldn't say what he needed and so I guessed. I was wrong. My mind – the result of clinical depression – still whispers to me that our relationship is over, that I ruined everything, that there was no making things right. How does one make up a special day? I spend over an hour driving around Columbia and Lexington looking for a florist open on Sundays, an endeavor that proves fruitless. Then I remember The Fresh Market, a natural grocery store on Forest Drive. They have flowers and they're open.

I am already halfway there, just crossing over Harden Street, when I decide to turn around and pick Bryan up for breakfast at The Original Pancake House. We don't talk much in the car. While he waits for a table, a short wait for a Sunday, I am next door picking out a beautiful bouquet and a card with a peacock on it. I write how sorry I am and how I wish I could've known his mother, that she must've been a beautiful person. At the restaurant, I walk in carrying the large bouquet. Bryan is already seated, had already ordered my French Press coffee, what I always get when I'm there. He cries when he reads the card. I learn that a loving gesture is always appreciated, even a day late, and that getting so stuck in my own thoughts, a habit of us writer types, can also separate me from those I love.

I return home and am again confronted by the blank page, with the task of writing about Cassie. All day, the title of one of her poetry collections, *This is how honey runs*, pops into my mind, but I'm not sure what to do with it. As I sit, staring forlornly at my notebook, I can see Bryan out of the corner of my eye. If I ask him how to start, he will give me the condensed form of the King's speech in *Alice's Adventures in Wonderland*: "Begin at the beginning . . . and go on till you come to the end: then stop." Perhaps I feel a bit like Alice now, seeking guidance from numerous sources – books, articles, and my teachers. At least, instead of a cryptic caterpillar, I have Cassie with her gentle wisdom. Her answer would be to just begin writing without attaching myself to the outcome, to get out of writing with my head and write with my heart.

The following day, I meet Cassie for lunch at Basil Thai. It's a stressful day and I'm almost late to our meeting because I convinced myself I needed to steam clean the carpet about twenty minutes before I was supposed to leave. When I arrive, I recognize Cassie's car immediately – the bumper is covered in stickers with positive messages of peace and tolerance.

Inside, she is already waiting for me. When she spots me across the way, she smiles widely, a smile that always puts me at ease. We both decide to have Masaman, a mild curry with potatoes, onions, and cashews, though she chooses tofu for her protein and I choose beef. She tells me that this is a celebration lunch as both of our teaching semesters are ending.

"So," I ask her after our food arrives, "I was looking over the interview you did with me for your Literary Mama column, and I reread what you said when I asked you about your trajectory as an artist and how you manage such a level of tranquility. You mentioned losing, not in rejection but in wasting time in 'all the pout and drama about [your work].' Could you say more about the drama of writing?"

"When we understand the connection between trauma, healing, and writing, our first books are on that theme." She leans in closer to me, "Two things are happening. One, you are breaking silences. Two, you are establishing yourself as a writer. It's not just about how well you're writing but knocking down these two walls. Rejection feels like the walls are winning. It's necessary to do that work. For me, both walls have been knocked down. I write what I want to write instead of trying to make it as a writer."

"That makes sense," I say. "I almost see my writing process as a dance, a dance with myself when I'm trying to write. The word drama just really struck me. I was like, oh yeah, there's me staring at the page, and there's me being frantic, and me walking around doing unrelated things, and then me saying I don't want to do this. It's almost a frenzied, ritualized avoidance."

"And support is really important too. I think that you don't have the support that you need when you're first starting out and you don't have the recognition that you need and so you're bouncing back and forth thinking you're the only one who believes in yourself, which is really hard."

"I get that. Sometimes it feels like life intrudes too. I kept trying to start this essay, but life kept getting in the way."

She lays out another small bed of Jasmine rice on her plate and ladles the curry on top. "When we think about work/life balance, it's like there's work and there's life, but there's just a huge constellation of things and they all connect to each other. I mean, I've even really felt the difference I feel in terms of food and cravings and hunger. If my writing is going well, then I want a salad. It's weird how he body is connected to all this."

"I eat more junk food when I have writer's block," I look down at the table.

"That's a desire to numb it all and just not feel it. Whereas, when you're writing then the feelings are coming through the writing, and you can pick different things."

I smile, "I like this idea of a constellation because when I started writing this essay, it started becoming about me, which always happens – nonfiction. I started writing about why I couldn't write. I think of it as an either/or, like I should be writing instead of considering that these are things I need to take care of so I can write. So I can have the balance to write."

Her eyes light up, "It works the other way too. If you make the writing the priority, the other things tend to go more smoothly."

After lunch, I was glad I had taken notes. She said what I needed to hear. When she headed out, it was toward a future of continued writing and teaching – *Earth Joy Writing* will be published on April 22, 2015, Earth Day, and Cassie is continuing and expanding her work with Courage Beyond, a program serving military members and their families. Her work in trauma and as a creative coach will continue too. For me, I'm returning home to write and, hopefully, avoid the drama of writing.

My Nemesis and Me:
Susan Lenz on Wim Roefs

By Susan Lenz

Wim Roefs wasn't the first Dutch art dealer to set up shop in Columbia. There were at least two others before him.

The first I knew was Andy Van Dam. I don't know when he initially came to town but I remember meeting him ... in the way many women remember things from their own past: I was pregnant with my second son. So, it must have been early in 1990. Andy had a storefront on Devine Street. I loved the place at first glance. Artwork leaned against every wall and was stacked on all flat surfaces. Old World paintings in classic gold-leafed frames hung beside 20th century lithographs by all the luminary names in contemporary art. I was thrilled to have Andy as a new custom picture-framing client at my little business, Mouse House, even though at the time, Mouse House was nothing more than a hobby. Andy treated me like a friend, a peer, an insider. Andy's shop felt like the ticking pulse of the art world. There was an air of privilege. Andy always wore a smile. I liked him right away.

"The frame is often the pimp that sells the painting," Andy said more than once.

No insult was meant and none taken ... just directness, blunt, straight to the point. Andy could also laugh at himself, his sales pitch, the silly comments his clients voiced about matching a great painting to a cheap sofa. Politely, he'd spin a tale to make all the colors work well together, no matter what the hues.

Fortunately, Andy trusted my tastes and opinions on framing. He always paid on time and never haggled over my pricing. Not only did I like Andy, I respected him. He respected me, too.

Those long gone days were a tumultuous time in my life. That summer was hot and sticky. I was steadily gaining over sixty pounds during the pregnancy, but, more importantly, the coastal engineering company that hired my husband Steve three years earlier was going through a nasty merger. Career-wise, this was Steve's first job after finishing his PhD. His job was the reason we moved south in the first place. We came from Columbus, Ohio full of the expectations of professional adulthood after semi-sequestered years struggling through grad school, but our life in Columbia wasn't what either of us envisioned. Steve was more miserable than me carrying a ten-pound baby boy. By August Steve quit engineering to frame pictures with me at Mouse House. This was a major gamble.

Mouse House had never before needed to make a profit. We didn't know if it could hit the break-even point, much less support our little family. We had $5000 in the bank, earmarked for updating Steve's resume, selling our house, and moving us to some far, far away place in the coming year. Something went wrong. It always does.

The snag came in the form of an opportunity. We learned of a forgotten stash of antiquarian prints, the remains of James Thornton Gittman's Ye Old Book Shop, a Columbia business that started right before World War I and lasted for nearly fifty years. Gittman's family tried to keep selling books and prints after his 1951 death, but it was hard and eventually failed. Jack Scoville, Sr., an interior designer and USC faculty member and his World War II veteran friend Hugh Fenzel purchased what was left. They intended to use the prints in Jack's residential work and to sell others through Hugh's antique mall booths. Something went wrong. It always does. The stash went into storage for years until, unexpectedly, Steve and I got to make an offer.

Of course, Steve and I knew next-to-nothing about antiquarian prints. We did know how to count. Hugh and Jack finally accepted our offer.

We called Andy Van Dam, our Dutch art dealer friend. According to Andy Van Dam, one ought not hire someone who wants "to buy" to assist with the pricing. Andy wanted a chance to buy. He made some telephone calls and then an important introduction. That's how we met Dr. John Bryan, a USC art faculty member and certified appraiser. Andy arranged a trade. We received ten hours of instruction with John Bryan. John Bryan received $750 dollars of our framing services.

Steve and I learned how to distinguish mezzotints, aquatints, dry point etchings, copper plate and steel engravings, and every manner of lithography while sitting at our own dining room table using a magnifying loupe to peer at the delicate marks made by the likes of Francis Bartolozzi, Luigi Rossini, and Sir Edwin Landseer's brother Thomas. We learned how to research works of art on paper, use the USC library reference books, and about past auction records.

This tumultuous time in our lives was one in which Andy Van Dam could have taken gross advantage of us. He didn't. He chose to educate us, respect our potential, and to be our friend. As far as I was concerned, Dutch art dealers had to be the most honorable, honest, and nicest people in any industry.

I've never known for sure, but maybe Andy's decision to leave town was influenced by another Dutch art dealer. I'll not mention this man's name. I have nothing nice to say about him. He had a slimy comb-over of thinning hair and reeked of sweat. His shirts looked as if they'd never seen the inside of a washing machine. His junker car limped down the street. He dropped Andy Van Dam's name as if a friend. He claimed to be taking over the antiquarian and fine art business where Andy left off.

There were some similarities between the two. Like Andy, this second Dutch art dealer knew quality artwork and had a good eye for antiques. He was direct to the point of rudeness, focused on the accumulation of wealth, and enjoyed the wheeling and dealing of retail. Yet, he had a habit of coming by Mouse House after hours and without a check book. He always asked for impossibly deep discounts. He offered false promises of more framing than I could handle and more money than I could spend. Instantly, I didn't like him. Neither Steve nor I trusted him.

Fortunately, he didn't last long. He skipped town, leaving an oil painting in our closet and a large, unpaid bill. I heard he owed hundreds of dollars to lots of people and took away plenty of artwork he hadn't actually purchased. In my mind, being a Dutch art dealer no longer had the same shiny luster.

Tumultuous times gave way to several years of constant work. Mouse House flourished and Steve's resume was never updated or mailed. A staff was hired. Taxes were paid. The kids grew up. I worked from the time I got up until I went back to bed. I missed being part of the art scene even though I went to just about every art exhibit in Columbia. Nothing was the same. There was no insider feeling like there had been in Andy's shop. No friendly conversation. No smile. I was just a picture framer, the person to whom real artists disliked owing money for the "pimp" to sell their paintings.

On Bastille Day 2001, I fired my head mat cutter and admitted (more to myself than to anyone else) that I wanted to be an artist when I grew up. I was forty-two and this story is another essay, one I wrote for the first volume of *The Limelight*. On those pages are paragraphs lauding my mentor, Stephen Chesley. It's all true, every word of it; but, where there's a mentor there is also a nemesis.

I heard about Wim Roefs over cups of coffee at Rising High in Five Points. A friend was artistically installing mismatched and random bits of tile in Wim and Eileen Roefs' downstairs bathroom. The cost was to be a fraction of new material and the result was to be as fantastical as Gaudì's mosaics in Barcelona. Another friend complained that Wim Roefs insulted her craftsmanship bluntly to potential clients. He was known to have a great deal of knowledge on the topic of art, especially African and African-American art.

Maybe I was distracted, especially when finally being introduced to Wim Roefs. Tall, dark, and (no, not exactly handsome) but in my mind brilliant is even better. My introduction, however, came long after first bumping into Wim.

Frankly, I thought Wim Roefs was German. He was making arrangements to show two dozen or so over-sized posters … original art … made by German artists from Columbia's sister-city Kaiserslautern. One of the local artists involved asked if I could provide 40" x 60" pieces of foam-centered board. I agreed, on the condition that I got the sheets back after the exhibit. When I dropped off the sheets, a man told me that they weren›t perfect but would have to do. To him, I was just a delivery person, certainly not a volunteer or a budding artist. There was no "thank you" and nothing was ever returned.

I'd just met Wim Roefs.

In 2004 Wim Roefs curated *South Carolina Birds* at the Sumter County Gallery of Art. There was a slick catalog. Over eighty works by forty-three living South Carolinian artists were included. Everyone I knew was talking about the show, the excitement of it, the honor of being included or the insult of being overlooked. Steve and I went to the opening reception. One of the artists Wim now represents introduced Steve to a friend saying, "He's Susan's husband. You know her. She does fiber thingies." Steve was polite but his ears burned. I didn't even get to speak to Wim Roefs. He was too busy talking to important people.

It was a beautiful show though. Beautiful and conceptually strong, from William Jackson's pre-historic sculpture *Raptor* to Janet Orselli's grass mattress and box spring coiled nest installation called *Sanctuary*. I adored the exotic dancer wearing Loren Schwerd's colorful, wing-inspired costume of men's silk ties. Stephen Chesley's gigantic oil seemed alive with birds hiding in their treetop abodes. There were images of eggs and suggestions of feathers. Birds never looked better. I couldn't help but admire the man who pulled it together. Silently, a goal was starting to form in the back of my mind: *One day I'll make work that is good enough ... good enough for Wim Roefs.*

Such a goal was quite lofty. For one, Wim Roefs hadn't noticed me enough to extend an invitation to a few select art sales he was conducting in his home. Artists involved told me, "just come"; but when I arrived, all the relatively affordable art had already been purchased. There had been a more exclusive preview party a night earlier, something for the elite, real art aficionados. This only made me more determined to earn Wim's respect.

Wim did talk to me during one of these home sales. He introduced me to an older man from whom he was trying to disengage himself. "This is Susan Dingman, a local picture-framer. She works at Mouse House and can probably tell you how that painting might look framed." I shook the gentleman's hand, said a few words, and quickly departed.

To the best of my knowledge, Wim Roefs had never been to Mouse House or had a reason to think of me as a picture framer. I was trying so hard to be an artist, not a framer. I was also using my birth name, Lenz. Yet, the man I most wanted to impress pawned me off on some geezer using my day job. Later, I cried. I always cry before summoning the strength to double up my efforts.

Work harder! Dig deeper! Strive for better quality ... conceptually with expert craftsmanship! Put in more hours! Damn it! Improve! Impress Wim Roefs! These were the things I told myself. These phrases became my action plan; the taste of salt a reminder; Wim Roefs my motivator.

My extra efforts were paralleled in Wim Roefs. From exclusive evenings in his Lee Street house, he moved to two-week engagements at Gallery 80808. Wim collected a stable of talented artists. He had pedestals and portable walls built. His exhibits were carefully curated and included slick catalogs. Wim's background in journalism resulted in great publicity. I was awed by every show. Wim personally manned each one from 11 AM until 7 PM, seven days a week.

As much as my admiration grew, my fledgling ego shrank as Wim's sales pitch soon drifted over the gallery wall into my little rental studio at Gallery 80808. During *Construction Crew II*, Wim's December 2006 exhibit, I couldn't help but overhear him say to a potential client: "Life is too short to sell bad art. Actually, life's too short to make bad art."

My blood boiled in silence. Neither Wim nor the other man knew I was stitching quietly nearby. I tried hard to reason out the conversation's punch-in-the-stomach shock. In my gut, I knew that without the freedom to create "bad art", nothing new and exciting would ever happen. "Good art" doesn't simply flow from the brush of a talented painter or sing from the strings of a brilliant violinist. Good art requires bad art.

I resented the misrepresentation. I wondered about Andy Van Dam, his ability to spin a tale, his mercantile manners, the blunt Dutch ways. In part, I understood my distaste. But reasoning didn't accomplish agreement nor did boiling blood hold my doubts at bay. True or false, my insecurities flared. Conviction kicked in. I'd just have to work harder.

During *Laura Spong at 80: Warming the Chill Wind with Celebration,* a show Wim organized, I heard his high pressure sales pitch again. "Laura, she sure can paint! It's too bad the inferior artists around here insist on hanging their work beside hers." The conversation went on with examples from past, annual exhibitions in which my work frequently hung beside Laura's. I was horrified and embarrassed even though my name was never directly referenced. Pulling my threaded needle through fabric, I cried and mentally doubled up my dedication to additional hours. Without even knowing it, Wim Roefs was providing plenty of conviction. By this time, I knew I had a nemesis.

For a while, I thought the best way to interact was to seek his advice. Little did I know that his arts education was no better than mine. I don't have any formal training. Neither does he. His undergraduate history degree from Radoud University Nijmegen included one independent study art history course. Yet, brilliant, highly confident, self-taught experts oozing strong opinions are people I generally put onto pedestals. Their worldly wisdom holds much more merit than spoon-fed academic advice.

So, in April 2006 while Wim sat at Gallery 80808 manning one of his exhibits, I asked for help pricing *Blues Chapel*. It was my work for Artista Vista, the next show to occupy the gallery. I didn't know how to price the installation. Theater curtains hung in my studio hiding everything except the twenty-four portraits of early female Blues singers. Bessie Smith's voice hung in the air. Votive candles and a music stand suggested an altarpiece. The atmosphere had viewers immediately lowering their voices to mere whispers despite the fact that no signage required any sort of silence. How does one price such a thing?

We sat at the lunch table. Wim mused on about high brow installations in New York City and Europe. He dropped names I didn't know. He mentioned galleries specializing in this sort of work, places that represent artists with proper degrees and university postings. I felt small and insignificant before he provided numbers.

Paraphrasing Wim's answer: "Individually ... retail prices ... $225 at the very most. But, I'd keep the twenty-four together ... if you can afford to wait. Add up the individual prices and then knock off 20%. That would be about the right price for your work. Oh, and ... you might be able to get someplace to show it ... like Pickens County Museum of Art. I had my Bird Show there. It's a nice place."
Thankfully, I'm a rather good actress. I hid my surprise, thanked him, and added, "If you can sell it for that, I'll pay you your standard 50% commission." I went back to my

studio and cried. Everyone told me that Wim encouraged artists to have more confidence in their work, charge more rather than less. Yet, $225 ... retail? At the most? Quick work with a pencil and paper: $225 times 24 minus twenty percent. $4320 retail or $2160 after commission. Seriously? For the next few weeks, I simply said, "I haven't come up with a price." I was afraid of looking like an arrogant fool, too in love with one's own art, to list it higher than Wim's recommendation. I was equally unwilling to part with the work for the amount he suggested. It just had to be worth more.

There wasn't time to wallow in depression. Karen Watson came to Artista Vista and invited the work to be shown at the Sumter Gallery of Art later in the summer. This would be my first museum solo show. At this juncture, however, I really did have to list a price ... at least for insurance reasons. Mentally, I revisited my conversation with Wim. He was right about one thing. The work was certainly stronger as a whole. I settled on $7,500. After all, Wim sold individual paintings for more.

Wim was also right about contacting Allen Coleman at the Pickens County Museum of Art and History. I knew Allen from the museum's annual juried art show. A year earlier, I'd received the juror's award for an altered book. Submitting a proposal was an active way for me to counter-balance the insult of Wim's pricing, a way to say, "My work is better than you think." I got the solo show in Pickens ... and one in Edgefield's Discovery Center ... and eventually one at the Greater Denton Art Council in Texas where I was paid more than Wim's figure for just bringing it there.

Although I started out seeking Wim's advice, my mind was changed after a few occasions when he offered it without me asking. One afternoon Wim explained how I ought to frame my "In Box" and "Stained Glass" series. Apparently, my years at Mouse House didn't render me qualified. He told me what sort of picture framing moulding I ought to use. Again, I was hurt. Again, I took action to counter-balance the humiliation. I entered the piece to which Wim pointed into Palmetto Hands, a juried fine crafts exhibit in North Charleston. It won an outstanding merit award, an amount more than the price tag.

A year later, Wim came into my studio and told me that I ought to raise my prices on these pieces but added, "after Eileen and I get one." Now, that puzzled me. I wasn't sure what to think but I knew exactly what to do. As soon as Wim left, I pulled off the price tag and raised it by $100. Ten more pieces sold within the next six months. I have Wim Roefs to thank for the extra thousand dollars.

The prices have gone up since then. This work got me several solo shows, representation at the Grovewood Gallery in Asheville, and into last year's Philadelphia Museum of Art Craft Show. I've wholesaled to galleries all over the country, including the American Visionary Art Museum in Baltimore. Amusingly, five pieces were selected for last year's 701 Center for Contemporary Art biennial, a place Wim Roefs helped co-found, a place he ran as a volunteer executive director for its first few years and now chairs the board.

I was proud to be included in the biennial. There was a subtle vindication in finally having art in 701 CCA. It opened in

October 2008 with an inaugural exhibit called *Textile Tales*. The entire first year had programing and exhibitions focusing on the legacy and materials in the textile industry, a way of paying homage to the building's past as the former historic mill village's community center. One would think that the core group spear-heading 701 CCA into existence and scheduling fiber artwork exhibits would want to reach out to all fiber artists in the immediate area. Wasn't I a working fiber artist? Didn't Wim Roefs at least know this? Had I not managed to become a blip on his radar?

Apparently not. In 2008 I wasn't even asked for my mailing list or whether I was a member of any local fiber, quilt, or textile groups. Instead, a last minute closing party for *Textile Tales* was scheduled for Friday, January 9th, 2009, the same evening as my reception for *Cyber Fyber*, an exhibit on which I'd worked for a year and had listed on every local Internet calendar including the one for Gallery 80808 where Wim's shows were also listed.

I was pretty torn up by this, but not in much position to complain, especially since 701 CCA was just about to initiate its art residency program with Ellen Kochansky. I met Ellen during the previous summer ... back when my *Blues Chapel* opened in Pickens, her hometown. She stood waiting to talk to me. We shook hands. She introduced herself. I nearly fainted. Ellen talked about her upcoming residency, about fibers as the focus for 701 CCA's first year. The truth is, I had no idea what she was talking about at the time. This was the first I'd heard of these great plans. I wasn't a blip on 701 CCA's radar. I wasn't a blip on Wim Roefs' radar. I'd made progress as an artist but not a dent in my quest for Wim's approval. Instead, Ellen was coming to town and I owed my gratitude to Wim for making it possible.

During Ellen's time in Columbia, I learned plenty but the most important thing was her advice on dealing with a nemesis. Ellen said that if I could, once-and-for all, rid myself of any and all negative feelings, I'd be making room in my heart to be filled with all the positive energy I was seeking. If I could just stop caring about Wim Roefs and wanting his approval, I'd have all the validation I'd ever need. I've been working on this ever since and making more headway than I thought possible. Gallery representation all over the country, a lengthy resume, solo shows, publications ... generally outside South Carolina's state lines ... were all to become mine. When seeking opportunities, it was easier in distant places, easier without the looming specter of a nemesis I was trying to forget.

Getting rid of a nemesis is a tall order, as impossible as my initial goal to earn his respect. I try constantly but it's a battle with myself. As my career grew so did my admiration for Wim Roefs. He's served as juror for just about every annual exhibit within a one-hundred mile radius, curated *Red State Blues* for the Halsey Institute, mounted *Civil/Uncivil: The Art of Leo Twiggs* at City Gallery at Waterfront Park in Charleston, and positively changed the lives of several local artists through his strong advocacy and sales of their artwork. He's on the Art in Transit Advisory Committee of the Charlotte Area Transit System and is a frequent panelist for art discussion groups from Augusta to the Georgetown Library. His gallery continues to present fantastic shows and he's led 701 CCA to one of the state's premier locations for contemporary art.

Trying to find balance, I thought I'd do something nice for Wim to mark the first anniversary of if Art, his Lincoln Street gallery. I designed the inter-connected blogs that function as its website. Later I bought a few pieces of art. I regularly attend Wim's shows and, of course, compliment the high quality work. Wim has a unique ability to stage an exhibit. It is easy to sing the praises of excellent catalogs and tri-fold brochures produced to better represent high caliber artists. Compliments are easy enough to give, but they aren't way to earn a Dutchman's respect or banish a nemesis. Maybe it's a Dutch thing, an ability to size up a person on first glance and then stubbornly stick to that initial impression regardless of change or scandal or artistic growth. I had respect with Andy Van Dam from the very first introduction. The second Dutch art dealer saw the entire world's population as pawns to be played, as means to his own greedy financial end. There was no changing his mind about me or my mind about him. Finally Wim Roefs. I made no impression at all. Naively, I worked to change his mind. Like a moth to a flame, I got trapped in my desire for impossible validation and then further caught when trying to free myself from the web I'd spun.

Finally, my intention with this essay was to once-and-for-all get over Wim Roefs, to spill my guts and speak my mind, to empty the negative as Ellen Kochansky suggested and fill it with all the positive things about Wim Roefs. By admitting my mistakes, my silly obsession to earn one man's respect, and the impossible quest for his artistic validation, I would finally be free.

Four pages of questions in preparation for this essay were sent to Wim. It was turned into twenty-three pages of answers including a link to a satellite image of his boyhood home in Velden, complete with a description of which window had been his. I waded through an academic life in journalism that brought Wim to Columbia in January 1989 in pursuit of a master's degree. His thesis focused on the New York Times coverage of the conflict in Northern Ireland. His PhD research was on John McCray and his newspaper, the *Lighthouse and Informer,* but that degree was never finished. Freelance writing and academic publications gave way to a career in art. Despite the many paragraphs, virtually nothing was written on this transition.

I did, however, read plenty of footnotes. I enjoyed pages describing a few early art purchases, the Anton Heyboer etching that was the one that got away, and the names of world class artists in his personal collection and those he'd like to own one day. Wim's account of meeting and marrying Eileen is simply charming ... a $25 notarized license one weekday morning. They celebrate the day they met, even though neither knows exactly which day in November 1989 it was. Wim's greatest regret is the tanking economy and he regrets not having enough time to read.

He described one of his proudest accomplishments as "raising the bar for art, exhibitions, and galleries in Columbia," carefully adding that this might sound immodest ... but that "immodesty is no worse than false modesty." To me, it doesn't matter; it's the truth. Reading Wim's responses to my questions reminded me of days at Gallery 80808. Wim is jovial and kind to all sorts of people, even their children and pets. He's really a wonderful person to those he respects. I'm just not one of them.

As much as I'd like to say "I'm rid of this nemesis. I no longer care. I no longer want to impress him. I no longer need him to validate my work. He's not part of my mental anguish anymore." I can't. I don't really want to give up the struggle. I'm not a quitter. More importantly, I'd be lying if I were to say that my nemesis hasn't spurred me toward lofty goals, deeper commitment to art-making, and a conscious effort toward improved quality, concept, and overall craftsmanship. Having a nemesis like Wim Roefs is like having an unceasing nag coming from the back of one's mind. Nothing is ever good enough. Every day must be an upward push. I don't know if I would have worked as hard without Wim Roefs' contributions to the Columbia art scene and his assumption that my work wasn't good enough for inclusion. I don't know if I would be the artist I am today without this nemesis.

Wim Roefs would like to be remembered as "someone who consistently presented exhibitions of art that actually should be seen" because "most things that people ... refer to as 'art' doesn't necessarily need to be seen at all." He thinks mediocre artists have the right to enjoy their process and find therapeutic benefits in it but "the mere fact that someone manages to put paint on a canvas, and the paint subsequently doesn't fall off, doesn't mean that it needs to be inflicted upon the rest of us." He doesn't want to be remembered as part of "the insufferable hyping of inconsequential or even bad art that goes on consistently in Columbia."

I'd like to be remembered in much the same way, as someone who consistently created fine art, worthy of being seen. I'd like to think any hype buzzing around my exhibits was positively merited. Yet there's a big difference between Wim's hopes and mine. I'd rather be the one crying over an arrogant insult than dishing one out. I'd rather be licking my wounds and doubling up my efforts to succeed, striving for an inclusion that will never come, seeking opportunities beyond the city limits, doubting my own abilities, finding my own artistic path, and handling the insecurities that persist because I can't shake this negative force in my life. My nemesis has propelled me, driven me, and improved my work. I'm not sure I can continue without this tug-of-war. Maybe I need him? Undoubtedly, I'm deeply in his debt.

In spite of myself, I love you Wim Roefs.

The Art and the Artist: Boyd Saunders

By Rachel Haynie

Gifted. That Boyd Saunders was very gifted was my first impression, and that single adjective registered immediately, connoting far more than just the talent resonating within one of his original prints – an etching, lithograph or serigraph. It would be years later before I learned he was also musically gifted.

While I can't recall whether I knew the art first or the artist, and it's quite possible I encountered them simultaneously - at an art show, most likely at McKissick Museum, I quickly became aware that the two entities were mutually inclusive. Like the difficulty one can have in discerning the dance from the dancer, Boyd's creativity makes it tough to tell where the artist leaves off and the art begins. As I got to know him years later, I fully appreciated a question once posed by his late, great friend and colleague John O'Neil. O'Neil acknowledged that many knew Boyd Saunders, but wondered aloud how many knew the work of Boyd Saunders. Wish John were still with us; I would offer a belated answer: to know Boyd Saunders' work is to know Boyd Saunders.

Down on those sheets are many of his inspiring facets. His images are ripe with humanity and the artist's respectfulness for humanity and life – his artful responses imbued with the foibles and fragility that make life fun and fortuitous. Proof-positive that he is a gifted storyteller floats off those surfaces. Although he has taken on myriad topics, and in myriad forms, for many years his output centered around literature from the pen of William Faulkner. Three suites of images – informed by *The Bear, The Sound and the Fury,* and *Spotted Horses* – enlarged Faulkner's writings by illustrating both some of the easily-recognizable scenes, and sometimes scenes or characters less noted by contemporary readers. If his art on those Faulknerian topics had been available while I was enrolled in the Southern Lit course at the University of South Carolina, I would have comprehended them better – might not have defaulted to Cliff Notes. Boyd's work is that descriptive, that telling. He art takes viewers beyond the author's prose.

In choosing such content to inform his art, Boyd has exhibited respect – for fine literature and for the South, especially the Southeast – the region of his origins. His handling of fellow Southerners in his art visually amplifies that innate respectfulness. It is a trait of his I have often observed oozing from him, sometimes as he was speaking gently with a student or an art patron, other times, more animatedly, with a friend for whom he clearly had warm regard.

His mastery of art encompasses a number of extraneous elements: not only talent and technique, but then his innate thoughtfulness - just one of the home-grown characteristics that seems to have cropped up from his upbringing on the family farm, just 25 miles from Memphis. Thoughtfulness has enabled him to magnetize people. Once introduced, whether from an academic podium, around a lithographic stone, at a conference or exhibition, a music rehearsal hall, or the parking lot of a Methodist church, he is etched in your consciousness. Once a friend, always a friend.

His principal art form, printmaking, has tended his patience, letting this trait bloom. So how does art seed patience? Back to Boyd's chosen genre: Printmaking necessitates the practice of patience because each color that a print will take on gets laid down in its own layer. Each layer is hand-pulled. The artist must mesh all the layers together in a very intricate configuration. Mistakes mean setbacks of days, not to mention loss of costly materials. The imagination to conjure up, and the talent to draw the image first, then figure out how to pull it apart visually, so as to section off each layer, is complex work. Having enough cuss words to get through a protracted project is almost as important as having enough clean paper, new blades for the x acto knives, and fresh inks.

Told within the margins of his lithographs are revered Southern stories divulging the level of respect Saunders has for regional tradition and that Sense of Place other regions fall short of. The artist's treatment of his living subjects, both two-legged and four-legged, exposes his regard for life. The range of emotions he evokes with inks and just the right amount of pressure permeates into fiber-laden papers discernable waves of forlornness and impending misfortune, and the fun and inter-activity of looking at a scene and knowing what must have happened before and what probably is going to happen after. The talent is unmistakable, even to an untrained eye, because the details are so precise, the proportions and perspectives so exact, and the techniques so polished.

Storytelling is communication. And teaching is communication. As a teacher, now a University of South Carolina Distinguished Professor Emeritus, his effective instruction was predicated on his willingness to be a role model for his students. Allowing his work to be seen, even in its stages of development, whereas many artists prefer to hold their work back until it is completely polished, set an example, exhibited his processes, exposed him to artistic vulnerability.

Inherent in the process of printmaking is the character-building willingness to delay gratification because there are so many steps and stages required for pulling a successful print.

This form of art is associated with another quality: flexibility. Once Boyd has etched an image onto a surface – sometimes an etching plate, sometimes a lithographic stone, he can tweak the image and change out the pigments used, but most importantly, he can make more prints. The greater the number of prints pulled from a single image, the more affordable for the public's art collectors, thus printmaking retains its centuries-old status as a populist art form. Being representative of the people's art form makes Boyd's originals as gregarious as he is.

From his earliest days in the USC Art department, Boyd's work got out and about. He showed his work in the print studio, at McKissick Museum on the USC campus, and at other student-accessible exhibition spaces. But the oft-lauded works also made their way into commercial galleries as well as exhibition walls - around Columbia, in Greenville, Aiken, Clemson, Spartanburg and Hilton Head, and beyond. Work has been on view in the nation's capital, Huntsville and Auburn, Alabama; Emory, Georgia; Houston, Texas; Jonesboro, Arkansas; Fort Wayne, Indiana; and Hilo, Hawaii. Last summer, his work returned to Oxford, Mississippi, close to the Ole Miss campus where Boyd earned his M.F.A. The solo exhibition at Southside Gallery coincided with the dates of the annual international Faulkner and Yoknapatawpha Conference.

My love of travels makes me appreciate that Boyd's art has been his passport to exhibit, and as often as possible, to travel to other countries to talk about the art, and to teach. He RSVP'd Yes, he'd be willing to show in The Netherlands; Buenos Aires; Argentina; Palazzo Venezia, Rome, Italy; and Beijing, China. He returned again to that Eastern country in 1995 for a series of lectures, exhibitions and an etching workshop for a dozen of Shanghai's top artists. Another might have felt out of place, first by towering over workshop participants as the lanky artist did, but also out of sensitivity to tradition. Imagine an American printmaker coming into an ancient culture to teach venerable artists an age-old medium that, for some reason, was not being practiced widely in China at that time. In that setting he became more of a mentor and friend than an academic-style professor. Thousands of miles away, he demonstrated his hallmark Lead from Within.

That style of leadership had been manifested many times, but perhaps none more effectively than in his founding and sustaining of Southeastern Graphics Council. Once he brought together his cohorts in the Southeastern College Art Conference in 1972, he has supported the organization actively and intrinsically, through a couple of name changes and progressive iterations, for more than four decades. In Spring 2014 Boyd attended the 42nd annual conference, this year in San Francisco, California. The organization's growth in importance and membership fully warrants its contemporary name: Southern Graphics Council International.

Abroad, as at home, he has been a role model in countless other ways, from his start here. His 1965 hiring, by the late Edmund Yaghjian, then chair of the University of South Carolina Art Department, came with a leadership requisite. Boyd was charged with establishing a print studio and "selling" not just the courses but the importance and value of the medium. The public, at this point in history, had exhibited readiness to own art, but was scrapping along in a fiscal climate where oils and even original works on paper were out of the mainstream's economic reach. Boyd was youthful, having been out of graduate school only a few years years, and was zealous to print. At Southwest Texas State College where he taught immediately after completing his terminal degree at the University of Mississippi, he had not been given free rein to produce his own prints. He got off the plane in Columbia, champing at the bit to allow ink to leach under his fingernails here, and with teaching experience enough to know students would follow him into the studio.

Those who studied with him between the mid-60s and the arrival of the new millennium still speak with admiration about the sense of community he established in the print studio - which got moved around multiple times in those early years. Regardless of its location, it was a great hang-out place for art majors as well as outsiders who chose printmaking as their required art class. It was his students who anointed him the Patron Saint of Second Chances. Some downtrodden students with abundant art talent - disavowed at other institutions of learning - had descended into deep funks because they believed those who had scolded them, told them they couldn't make decent art. Boyd engineered Roads Back for countless students who couldn't see their innate worth or their own paths until he coaxed them into showing him what they were capable of. He has been an unswerving practitioner of his own policy: Praise loudly; criticize softly.

Flexibility gives tenacity its tensile strength. And tenacity through flexibility is another admirable attribute Boyd personifies. His raw refinement camouflages a deep reality: recent years have been a tough row to hoe. So it is the grace with which he has handled adversity that caps my admiration for him. Rossville, Tennessee farm life cultivated his ability to shoulder difficulty. As family was his leaning post in those formative years, they also were when he began facing great uncertainly nearly two decades ago. His "built" community brought students into that circle of family.

So, tenacity, such as he had modeled for students, came around full circle and gave him a leg up following brain surgery in 1995 to remove a walnut-sized tumor that tried to warn him of trouble by numbing his face and putting a bad taste in his mouth. When the tumor didn't easily show itself, Boyd set up shop at the Medical University of South Carolina library and searched on his own until he found references that made sense. As he was undergoing delicate brain surgery, students, faculty and other friends anxiously waited for medical updates, from Columbia to California. He survived the brain surgery, but as a result, lost vision and hearing on his left side.

Healing and adjustments were underway when unrelated back troubles sent him back to doctors. When a pharmaceutical was prescribed for his back, he asked persistently before taking the medication: "Does this drug have any side effects?" Four times he was told no. But the pressure response the drug had on his eye profoundly affected his vision. Now his "good eye" was also damaged.

Many tribulations later, it was his students who rallied around him when he was still struggling to get his brain to start talking again to his hands. A few loyals showed up at his home and studio in Hilton, near Lake Murray, and convinced him he could, and should, finish a suite of prints they felt had languished long enough. In his characteristic gentility, he acquiesced, taking off their shoulders the shroud of helplessness, and let them lead him back to his work table where they pitched in and helped him restart The Sound and the Fury, which became one of his most acclaimed suites of work.

When he first was well enough to return to his classroom, his energy supply often was sapped before any class period ended. More revealing, more accurate than any written semester-end evaluation, the behavior of Boyd's students' gave testament to his professorship. Students stepped up and helped, in whatever way was needed, enabling him to continue teaching.

Now, as then, students have kept their places – by his side. I watched as a former student waited at the back of the gallery to speak with Boyd following his 2011 art lecture at Columbia Museum of Art, part of "An Artist's Eye: A Journey through Modern and Contemporary Art", curated by his great friend, Sig(mund) Abeles. The student's smile said he knew once the crowd dispersed, Boyd would find him, acknowledge him, that his mentor would make time for him. If ever you were in the fold of Boyd Saunders, you remain in that fold. That, about Boyd, inspires and motivates me, and it affects so many others in similar ways.

Gradually, by the grace of new science, Boyd has made his way back from much of the vision loss, exhibiting along that frightening and grueling journey strong evidence of great Southern bearings, even when a cane in one hand hampered his usual glad-handing and shoulder clapping. In those now-gone days, walking took both hands. The first held the cane; the second hand was on the elbow of whoever was leading the way. He still calls his wife Stephanie A Rock for the faithful structure she provided then and continues to provide, as she has throughout their long marriage.

As Boyd was reclaiming himself, he had one genre that kicked in like good insurance, a fall back he could rely on until he could fully return to his studio and the visual art that has dominated his professional career. As storyteller, Boyd is an impresario, as indefatigable as he is with art output. Through his art and from his Southern tradition of oral lore he summons tales and anecdotes he has stocked up like shelved provisions in a country store, and he brings them down and sets them on the counter for dispensing when the occasion is right. If you think you've heard one before, you haven't because he has changed the context, making it new.

As another rendition of storytelling, he often adds bits of text - narrative or verse - to his art, reversing the example set by William Blake, the wordsmith believed to have been first to illustrate poetry.

Within the funny elements of storytelling, humor often is self-deprecating, the laugh never netted at another's expense. He says of himself: "I am not smart enough to do something half-way." Yet even that dig is only half self-deprecating because it divulges his predilection for thoroughness, just another birthright from his family.

The gentility of his voice and his well-honed vocabulary draw listeners close to him for fear of missing something of value. Sometimes the tenor voice tells its story in actual notes and music. Over his years here in the Midlands, he has sung with local choral groups, for several decades with the Palmetto Mastersingers.

To approach him, or be approached by him is to enter a rich realm where words and imagery intertwine, weaving together a safe zone, an incubator in which old traditions and ideas are turned freshly on their sides, a zone from which you depart somehow feeling better about yourself and the world you're navigating.

And I also really like the way he wears his hat.

More Than a Story: Homer "Pappy" Sherrill

By Michael Miller

I must confess, I wasn't feeling any undue excitement on the drive out to Pappy Sherrill's house that October afternoon in 1997. Pappy was an 82-year-old fiddler who'd been playing old-time country music around Columbia for so long, I'd begun to take him for granted. I was, however, rediscovering bluegrass at the time, thanks primarily to new music from the Del McCoury Band and Alison Krauss & Union Station. So I thought it would be fun to get Pappy's take on what the young pickers were up to.

Other than that, it was just another newspaper assignment, albeit one I'd suggested and volunteered to write. I felt I already knew as much as I needed to know about Homer "Pappy" Sherrill and his group, the Hired Hands. After all, I was a native Columbian. My grandparents had lived on Preston Street just a block away from Valley Park where every year a "shut-in picnic" was held for folks from nursing and retirement homes who were bused to the park for potato salad, sweet tea, and sandwich squares on light bread.

While the old folks sat and ate at picnic tables or in wheelchairs, Pappy, Snuffy Jenkins, Greasy Medlin, and the other Hired Hands would play hillbilly tunes between skits of slapstick comedy. My granddaddy would walk me down to the park every year, and we'd watch the shenanigans of the Hired Hands from the side of the stage.

Years later, I followed newer versions of the group after Snuffy and Greasy had passed away. These Hired Hands featured whiz kid banjo player Randy Lucas and his dad Harold Lucas on guitar. The group's music drifted a little closer to what was generally considered bluegrass, but there were still plenty of jokes and cuttin' up between the songs. Like I said, they had been around so long and played so often at events and gatherings, I thought I knew all about Pappy Sherrill and the Hired Hands.

But I didn't.

I had no idea.

I followed the directions Pappy had given me, and after meandering along some back roads between Chapin and Lake Murray, I came to an inviting and comfortable one-story house with a long porch across the front. It was nestled amongst a stand of pine trees, a relatively modern home made to feel like a rustic country lake house.

Pappy was waiting for me on the porch as I climbed out of my car. He waved, invited me inside, and offered me a seat in a spacious room with open windows and a cool breeze. He took a seat opposite, and I placed my tape recorder on a coffee table between us. There was a violin case in the chair next to Pappy not an arm's length away.

I thanked him for allowing me to come out to his home, and I related my memories of seeing the Hired Hands at the shut-in picnics. Pappy's eyes crinkled into a smile behind his glasses, and he said, yes, he remembered the shut-in picnics, too. And the radio shows. And playing to big crowds at The Township auditorium. And being offered a job by Bill Monroe.

"What? The Bill Monroe?"

I was suddenly perched on the edge of my seat.

"Oh yeah, I had a chance to go with Bill Monroe when he was wanting a fiddle player, but I never had a hankering to go," Pappy said. "That's a rough going. Those boys had a big bus to ride on, but I tell you, you leave your family for a month at the time, and the star makes most of the money. You make enough to get by and carry a little money home to pay your bills, but you don't make that much."

Bill Monroe, who died in 1996, is an American icon, the father of bluegrass music. The fact that he once asked Pappy to join his legendary group gave me pause. It raised my routine newspaper assignment to a much higher calling. It seemed Pappy Sherrill was more than just a long-time participant on South Carolina's music scene. He was an American icon, too, maybe not as renown as Monroe, but certainly one of his significant contemporaries. This was going to be fun, I thought, and I settled back into the big soft chair.

As we talked and laughed that afternoon, Pappy let the memories flow like a cool mountain stream. His voice was as soft and gentle as a feather pillow, and I realized I was in the presence of a humble, contented man who had played a much bigger role in the history of American country music than I ever imagined.

My "interview" with Pappy was no such thing. I remember asking a simple question, "When did you learn to play the fiddle?" and immediately forgetting all about my tape recorder, the time, and even the reason I was there. Pappy gazed out the screen door at the swaying pine trees and took me back through the years.

"I got a little fiddle out there on the porch, it's just about had it," he said. "It's just a piece of tin now. Santa Claus brought it to me when I was seven years old. My mother bought it for me. I learned to play 'Little Brown Jug,' 'Coming Around the Mountain,' stuff of that nature, old time mountain tunes out of the hills. 'Go Tell Aunt Patsy the Old Grey Goose is Dead,'" and his grin told me that was one of his favorites. "I could hear somebody play it and I could pick it up pretty quick. I had a good ear."

Pappy grew up in a place called Sherrill's Ford, a "wide place in the road" between Mooresville and Hickory in North Carolina where his family settled after emigrating from Scotland. "They forded the (Catawba) river right there at Sherrill's Ford. Dad was a farmer, and there were six boys in our family. Six boys and a girl. She worked the fields just like we did."

With his keen ear and nimble fingers, little Pappy, or little Homer I should say, attracted attention from the country folk with his fiddling. They encouraged Homer's dad to take him to Mooresville where he could get some lessons. So Homer and his dad hopped in the family's T-Model Ford truck and drove into Mooresville where they found a violin teacher named Dad Frank Williams, an old bachelor who lived in an apartment about the five-and-dime store. Little Homer started playing, and Dad Frank sat back, smiled and said, "Homer, you'll make a good violinist, you just practice good now."

So Pappy was on his way. He played in various string bands with his brothers, all the while listening to radio shows at night from Nashville, Chicago, and most importantly, the WBT Barn Dance from Charlotte. When Pappy's dad took a job at the furniture factory in Hickory and moved his family out of the country, it opened doors for Pappy and his string band aspirations. He called his group Homer Sherrill and the Crazy Hickory Nuts, and it wasn't long before a radio station over in Gastonia heard about the band and invited them to play a show on the air. It was 1928, and Pappy was only 13 years old.

"I took me and my brother and a couple more, and we went to Gastonia. We sat in chairs around one old box-type microphone, and it was just like we were sittin' around chewin' the bull. Back home, they could barely hear us, but they said they could hear 'Comin' Round the Mountain' and this and that.

"That was a great opportunity then. That was something, to think that we were 40 miles up the road and they could hear us at home. Great day alive!"

Opportunities came by the bushel after the performance on WSOC in Gastonia. Pappy and his Crazy Hickory Nuts began playing all around the region, and in 1934, they were invited down to Charlotte to audition for the WBT Barn Dance. The big time!

The Barn Dance was sponsored by Crazy Water Crystals, a laxative company. Stars of the show were Charlie and Bill Monroe, with other bands on the bill such as a group from Harris, N.C., called the Jenkins String Band that featured a fun-loving banjo player named Dewitt "Snuffy" Jenkins.

Crazy Water Crystals sponsored other radio shows around the Carolinas and Georgia, too, and when they liked what they heard from Pappy and his Hickory Nuts, they offered them a noontime show in Asheville on WWNC. But after a while, Crazy Water Crystals pulled out of the smaller markets, and it might have left Pappy and his pals high and dry if they hadn't struck up a friendship with some folks from the JFG Coffee Company in Knoxville.

"We changed our name to John, Frank and George: The Good Coffee Boys and broadcasted a good while there out of Asheville. But, man, it was tough. We had to send our clothes home to get 'em washed. Two of the fellows went back to Hickory, said they couldn't stay up there anymore."

I sat back in my seat as the late afternoon breezes lifted the curtains and Pappy meandered through the years. One of his groups, the Blue Sky Boys, took over for Charlie and Bill Monroe at WGST in Atlanta for a while after the Monroe Brothers got tired of the big city and moved back to Charlotte. Next it was on to Raleigh as The Smiling Rangers, then to Danville, Va., then all of a sudden Crazy Water Crystals went out of business and Pappy was out of a job.

"So I moved back to Hickory," Pappy said. "Just took it easy for a while, did little things around the house."

But he started tuning in a radio show from Columbia on WIS called "Byron Parker and The Hillbillies" that featured Snuffy Jenkins on banjo and two guitarists, George "Sambo" Morris and Leonard "Handsome" Stokes. Pappy liked what he heard. Then one day the announcer, Byron Parker, said the group's fiddle player, Snuffy Jenkins' brother Verl, was suffering health problems and wouldn't be touring with the group. The rest of the Hillbillies, however, would soon be coming to a town near you.

"He said they were coming to the Granite Falls School, up above Hickory. I thought I'd go up there and hear them. I threw my fiddle in the trunk and went up there," Pappy said.

Snuffy recognized Pappy from the Barn Dance in Charlotte, and he introduced him to Byron Parker. Parker asked Pappy if he'd brought his fiddle. "Yeah, I always carry that," Pappy said. "It's my bread and butter."

Parker told Pappy to resin up his bow and practice a couple tunes with the group. "I got through playing and he said, 'We'd love to have you.'"

So Pappy and his wife moved to Columbia in 1939 and Pappy became part of the WIS Hillbillies. (They became the Hired Hands in 1948 in honor of their long-time friend and emcee, Byron Parker, who died that year. Parker would close every radio show with, "And now until we meet again, either in person or on the air, this is your old hired hand Byron Parker saying goodbye, good health, and God bless you every one.")

For the next 51 years, Homer Sherrill and Dewitt Jenkins would entertain thousands. When Pappy started being identified by fans as the old-man character he played in a radio skit, he just went ahead and took the name "Pappy." From then on it was Pappy and Snuffy, an artistic relationship that turned into a deep friendship.

"Old Snuffy," Pappy said with a fondness that stretched back over the years. "Snuffy had them big shoes. He'd wear them on the wrong feet and have those baggy pants. He was a prince of a fellow. He beat anything I ever saw in my life."

Snuffy was 81 when he died in 1990 after a long fight with cancer. His daughter asked Pappy to play Snuffy's favorite him, "Whispering Hope," at the funeral.

"Snuffy always liked that one," Pappy said. "A tear came to the corner of my eye while I was playing, but I couldn't help it."

We sat in silence for a moment, then I realized it was getting late and I needed to head back into town. I thanked Pappy for everything, the stories, the history, and the inspiration. I told him I was going to pull out my guitar when I got home and play "Step It Up and Go," "Coming Around the Mountain," and "Wabash Cannonball." I might even try "Go Tell Aunt Patsy the Old Grey Goose is Dead."

"Let me play you one before you go," he said, and he opened his case and took out his prized fiddle from 1811. "This one's called 'Wednesday Night Waltz.' They don't play 'em like this anymore."

Pappy caressed the fiddle's neck, drew the bow across the strings, and sent beautiful music around the room, out across the porch, and into the treetops. I was mesmerized by the 82-year-old's calm, soulful dexterity, and I can hear that fiddle tune to this day.

My story on Pappy appeared in the newspaper on Sunday, Oct. 19, in 1997. A few days later, I received a small card with a handwritten note of thanks from Pappy, who said he'd enjoyed talking to me and really liked "the write-up in the paper."

Four years later in November of 2001, the phone rang on my desk. It was a friend calling to say that Pappy had died a few hours earlier. I put the phone down and sat there quietly for a few minutes and let my mind drift back through all those stories of barn dances, hillbilly comedy, and radio shows. I remembered Pappy playing "Wednesday Night Waltz" and how it seemed to make time stand still. A tear came to my eye while I was sitting there at my desk. I couldn't help it.

There's Still Some Room at the Table: George Singleton

By William Garland

I don't have a personal relationship with George Singleton, and I don't have any deep insight into his inner psyche. If that's the kind of essay you were hoping to read, there is a pretty good chance you'll walk away from this one disappointed. I had hoped that I would somehow find myself sitting across from George at a bar that wasn't like a bar in Spartanburg, but like one of the ones that only exists because he wrote it into existence. I liked to imagine that we would be talking about coyotes in the suburbs, Taylor Grocery, the new old label on Miller Lite cans, and the other topics that circle in-and-around conversations when writers sit down to talk to one another. We'd sit there and shoot the shit until somebody needed us to help rig up a wench to pull this out-of-towner's vehicle out of a creek. And that'd give me the story. I don't know what that story would be, but there would be a story there, and there couldn't help but be insight buried down in it.

But as it is, I'm just a fan. I haven't had the chance to sit across from him and figure out what he thinks about the Miller Lite cans or any of the other significant issues of our day. In fact, I've only met George once. It was at the end of the weekend at the South Carolina Book Festival. He was set up at one of those big tables to sign books, and in another fifteen minutes the doors were all closing and the lights were going out.

So maybe I'm not the writer that should be talking to you about George Singleton. I'm sure that other people could fill these pages with colorful anecdotes and touching tributes. I can't give you those.

But this is what I can give you. This is what I do know about the man that shaped a little part of every short story I ever sat down to write. Prior to that day at the book festival, I'd only been on the periphery of an email correspondence, where my name was thrown in the mix with a few of the editors at *Yemassee*. We were all asking him to judge a short story contest for us. Like most grad students, we were just impressed that a well-published writer agreed to work with us at all. I think we more-or-less assumed that we'd send along the finalists and then a few months later, we'd get some cryptic message scrawled out on a napkin with the shorthand names of the winning stories and, if we were especially lucky, the one ultimate winner would be underlined and circled.

Instead, we got an email two days later with detailed critiques of each of the thirteen stories, and a long message thanking us for giving him the opportunity to read so many great short stories and to have the chance to, as he said, "pay it all forward." After that, he was a saint in our eyes. The editors gathered at Goatfeathers that evening and drank our drinks and raised our bottles to him and our contest winners. The evening turned into late night, and we all sat around the back table laughing about one of his critiques and trying to figure out how he could possibly know about the proper way to wrestle down an alligator, but I kind of thought that was where it all ended. And I guess it was until I met him two years later at that book-signing table right before the doors locked and convention hall staff started breaking everything down to prepare for the next event.

It didn't take him more than two seconds after hearing my name to say, "I know you. We worked together on that short story contest a few years back." And for the next ten minutes, George Singleton talked to me like we were old friends. We might not have gotten around to the big topics of our day or been called on to live out the events of one his short stories, but for those next few minutes, he stood there and joked around with me about Wofford, Columbia, and that terrifying moment when we you can no longer call yourself a grad student. He stole a brochure from Brian Carpenter and wrote down the names of magazines and journals where he could find my stories.

I don't know if he went back and read any of my work, and I'm not sure if it matters. What does matter is that George Singleton knows how to make an aspiring writer feel like he's already got a place at the table. That's what I walked away with that day. There's a chance that I'll never be able to write a short story that exists on the page the way that Singleton's do, but I knew then that I could be grow into the kind of writer that knows how to make the table bigger and the conversation richer.

A Man, a Tam, and a Guitar: Drink Small, the Blues Doctor

By Clair DeLune

The New South Music Hall was dark, cavernous and loud. Everyone was there to see the hottest band in South Carolina, The Brother Band, which featured five of the handsomest men in the region, including two blistering Blues-Rock lead guitarists, dual powerhouse drummers and a long, lean and lanky blond lead singer and bassist providing the bottom end. That should have been sufficient to keep a girl's eye from wandering, but what this girl noticed was off stage.

Ambling through the crowd of lithe, boisterous, college-aged barflies was a quiet, short, stocky man in a dark suit, wearing a tam-o'-shanter hat and carrying a guitar.

I began a conversation with Drink Small, the Blues Doctor. It would not be my last.

There were many opportunities to see and hear Drink Small perform live as the years went passing by. Admiration grew to deep respect, then to friendship. The seed planted from that first conversation in the early 1970s took root during his many appearances on WUSC-FM's Blues Moon Radio, where he had a standing invitation as guest host each January in association with his birthday celebrations. He also has been a longtime honored guest speaker and performer for my various music history and appreciation courses at the University of South Carolina through the 1990s, including Blues History and most recently, as an esteemed guest as recently as January of 2013, for Music of the Carolinas.

"She's not only my wife, she's my nurse for life."

After a long courtship, Drink married Andrina, who is known to her friends as "Drina," following the untimely passing of his only son in 2012. He confided that the time was right for him to marry because "I only want to have one wife, so I waited to marry until late in life."

Age has come with health challenges, and Drink considers Drina, who is a nurse, a Godsend, but she is also notable as the inspiration for three of the artists' best songs, "Fish Frying Mama," "The Nurse Song," and "A Good Woman is Hard to Find." With a vision impairment that progressed through the years to complete blindness in 2014, Drina has stood by Drink and has cared for him more and more.

Not long ago, Drina helped put together a surprise for Drink. He was invited to play and speak about Piedmont Blues for my Music of the Carolinas class at USC in January 2013. Because he plays so many styles, he was able to demonstrate what makes Carolina and Virginia Blues distinct from other styles. As a true "songster," he engaged the students by singing most of his lecture, creating expressive songs off the top of his head – which still boasted a tam, just as he did on the first night we'd met forty years prior.

When his lecture concluded, and the students had run out of questions for him, he put aside his silver-topped steel guitar after playing the last of many encores. Drina and I wheeled out a cake and ice cream to celebrate his 80th birthday to his surprise and delight. He regaled the class with story after story, and yet another generation of fans was born.

After class, Drina and Drink guest-hosted the Blues Moon Radio show and spoke about his much-lauded return performance at the Apollo Theatre in 2012 in memoriam for Howlin' Wolf's longtime guitarist, Hubert Sumlin. Drina said, "While Drink was performing, some fellow with a funny accent was very excited and asked me all about Drink."

As it turns out, that gentleman with the funny accent was none other than the iconic British "Blues God," Eric Clapton, who reportedly watched with rapt attention as Drink played.

Drink Small is a man of whom people take note. He's a man of letters, but he's most importantly a man of the people.

He loves to hear from his fans and friends. We've established a routine: I call almost every day to read the comments people leave on his Facebook page, "Drink Small, the Blues Doctor," and help him type his responses. We talk about his health and how he is doing. And sometimes he shares stories from his past. Many times, we laugh.

One such story was about another favorite Bluesman. Drink confided that sometime back in the '70s, he walked from his old house over on Lady Street, near Harden, to the Taylor Street Pharmacy, just a few blocks from Township Auditorium, to pick up some beer.

"A black man with a lantern jaw – you know… like Jay Leno's – stopped me," he said in his deep voice. "He asked me where he could find saxophone reeds. I told him there was a music store next to a pawn shop and I'd show him where. We went on down the road, got him his reeds, drank a few beers, and that night Bull Moose Jackson was able to do his gig at the Township because I helped him find reeds."

Drink explains why he believes the composer of hits such as "Big Ten Inch Record" (later covered and made a hit by rockers Aerosmith) and "Get Off the Table, Mabel, the Two Dollars is for the Beer," chose to reach out to him instead of one of the many others inside the pharmacy: "He must have seen my tam and known right away I was a musician."

"Life goes fast, and soon it is in the past"

He has lived a storied musical history. He has played at the Apollo in Harlem, NYC, twice; first with the Spiritual Aires, a gospel group he joined as a teenager back in the early 1950s in Bishopville, South Carolina, but most recently in tribute to Hubert Sumlin in 2012. He received the "Jus'Blues" "Bobby Blue Bland" award in 2013, and has twice been given the Key to the City of Columbia. He holds an honorary Ph.D. from Denmark Technical College, of which he is especially proud, because the Blues Doctor, who has studied both barbering and accounting, is now officially an honorary doctor of letters.

Across his more than eight decades, he has played for the Jazz and Heritage Festival in New Orleans several times, the Chicago Blues Festival and everywhere in between. His biography is about to be published by History Press; he was recently featured in the September 2014 issue of Columbia Living Magazine and is among many legendary Southern Roots artists in the featured line up of the Music Maker Relief Foundation's Roots Music extravaganza October 2014 fundraiser in Durham, North Carolina.

"I'm an initiator not an imitator."

Drink has influenced many people – fans as well as other musicians. From the start, he's played with many well-known stars, including Sister Rosetta Tharpe, "The Godmother of Rock & Roll," who took him on a regional tour in the 1950s and asked him to remain as her regular guitarist for her world tours. His roots in South Carolina have always been strong, and his personal style is so deeply ingrained that he wanted to focus solely on making his own style of music, so he returned to South Carolina and settled in Columbia, which was the hub, not only musically, but geographically, for his home state.

His style is unique, but is based upon the pentatonic style, in which it is common to play around the beat, not directly on it, as is typical in Eurocentric musical styles. There is a misperception of sloppiness or missed notes for those whose ears are not attuned to the Afrocentric style, but the music is intended to sound loose. Many have emulated that style and work hard to do what Drink does so freely and authentically. His music is about his life. He composes songs that are topical, such as "The United States Will Never Be the Same," which is about Barack Obama becoming the first black president, but although it speaks to the experience for the general public, the spirit of the song remains true to Drink's personal style – it speaks strongly about how it affects him.

"I had to go blind before I could really see – that's a true story because that person is me."

"My last name is Small, and my stature is not tall." Despite that, he has a huge effect on people he meets and entertains. He's completely blind now, but says that he "sees" things more clearly than ever.

He is famous for his "Drinkisms," which are short rhymes about life. "Drink Small Does It All" and "Tryin' to Survive at 75" are CD titles as well as Drinkisms, but his wry, savvy outlook on life runs deeper than mere couplets. As he has aged, he's become more philosophical and carefully tends his gospel roots because he wants to "get right with God before I get to heaven."

Blues Moon Radio pays tribute to artists who have made a major impact on the Blues through its "Artist of the Month" focus. The impact that Drink Small has had – and will continue to have – in music earned him the honor of being selected as Blues Moon Radio's first ever "Artist of the Year." Each week during the 25th silver anniversary year of the show, I have asked Drink to suggest two songs for the Blues Moon Radio playlist from his compilation of originals. Almost every week, he asks me to play, "Never Too Late to do Right," a song that gives a short rendition of the Prodigal Son story. With so many heartfelt messages in so many of his songs, listeners may wonder, "Why that one again?"

"I want to turn some hearts," Drink says. "And that will take a little work. I want this to be a hit. But not a Top 40 hit. I want to hit a million people's hearts with this song."

Drink has received many honors, homages and tributes through the years, but his fondest dream is to play for President Obama before the Commander in Chief completes his second term and leaves the White House. Nothing would make this legendary Carolina Bluesman happier than to sing for the president.

Despite being fully blind now, Drink Small can still envision that dream becoming a reality.

Knowing Drink for more than four decades has given me – and his many friends and fans from every generation – the ability to dream those dreams with him. We have every reason to work toward making that dream come true for him because, despite his advancing age, "it *is* never too late to do right."

Driving Toward the Desert: Paul Kaufman

By Chad Henderson

We're driving toward the desert.

The windows are halfway down, and the smell of sandy wind is flowing through the sports utility vehicle - on loan from Hertz or something...wait, being rented from Hertz or Enterprise. It's a rental car. Good, you haven't lost the ability to self-correct. There's music mixing with the varying cadence and volume of the wind, something from the 80s - very celebratory. "Let's Hear it for the Boys?" Whatever it is, we've already had a lot so we're singing every word. Well, I've had a lot. I can't speak for everyone because every person has their own definition of "a lot" - my definition is "whatever I had tonight." I use the word "whatever" because I can't remember what I had exactly. But here we are - driving toward the desert.

Paul is in the driver's seat, and the rest of us - all friends - are looking ahead of us. We're watching the landscape change as we coast ahead. Behind us Albuquerque grows dimmer against the black of the New Mexican night. There are still too many signs of electricity for us to stop. We said we wanted to go to the desert. We just completed a week of work which we had done well and professionally, and now we were celebrating and savoring in a land of stucco, cacti, and chilies. Paul is the Captain of this fiesta. And now we're driving out to the sand - sand for days.

Get a hold of yourself, boy. This is a first you're about to experience. You've never seen a real desert. You've loved the idea of deserts since you were a kid. The first time you saw Indiana Jones and the Last Crusade you loved watching that Paramount Pictures logo turn into a craggy mountain in the American west. The west felt like it didn't really exist back then - but it does. And you're in it. And maybe you shouldn't have had that last wine, or was it a beer? Maybe it was a liquor drink. I've had too much.

The buzz of civilization had been traded for the natural glow of the moon and a Lite-Brite of stars above. "I think we can pull over soon," Paul says.

We're driving toward the desert.

———

Paul Kaufmann is a theatre artist. I don't use that italicized word loosely. His mission to create, his range of experiences, and his allowance of the visceral married with the deeply considered in his theatrical work brings to fruit what can only be deemed the product of a theatre artist: meaningful and truthful expression.

Paul calls Columbia, SC home, but his work as a theatre artist has taken him from coast to coast, and abroad. From Off-Broadway performances in new works at LaMaMa to originating roles at theatre festivals in Wales and Romania, and from workshopping a script in Key West to traveling with it to an Australian production - Paul is always ready to try something new. He craves it. He pursues it.

Ask the patrons of Columbia's theaters and abroad or the participants in the ever changing local theatre community about Paul Kaufmann - and many will tell you he's a highly regarded actor. Others know him as a director, visual artist, designer, vocalist, and writer as well. Those who have been lucky enough to form a friendship with him will tell you he's a dear friend and a lot of fun. I'm one of these lucky people who can claim the latter. I'm also a theatre artist who gets the gift of collaborating with him.

I met Paul in 2006 when I was matriculating. I had been cast in a Restoration piece that claimed to be a comedy, but unfortunately the only part of the process that sported an iota of comedy was the laughter we shared over conversations with fellow castmates on breaks. Paul just so happened to be in this cast. I had enjoyed and admired Paul's work in a show I had seen a year before. I was nervous and excited to make the acquaintance of this actor I already respected, and, from what I understood, was respected by many of the faculty and the graduate class of actors. I was relieved to find out that he was affable. We became friends over the course of that process.

In the early part of the new millennium, Paul created an acting company that specialized in training and contracting actors who could believably portray children in forensic interview training classes. He was answering a call from the state government, which was seeking to improve their training effectiveness. His entrepreneurship deepened as he successfully turned the company into an LLC, and began developing contracts with other state governments and different federal agencies. I learned about this unique application of acting that Paul had been developing when we were working on that aforementioned theatre piece together. After the show had closed, I was humbled when he asked me to train and participate in a forensic training session that was coming up at the National Advocacy Center in Columbia. I'd be working for Paul's company who had been contracted by the FBI for this training.

As I began my orientation with Paul for my first time on the job, I found myself receiving the most influential approaches for instinctual existence during performance. To play a child realistically you had to be visceral. You had to be in the moment. You had to be truthful. Paul's coaching turned into practice as I walked into my first mock forensic interview.

The interviewer-in-training seemed to believe I was a child. For a minute or two I actually felt like a child. I believed myself. At that moment I understood what Paul's training had afforded me. It had a distinct impact on me as a growing actor and director. For the first time I realized what it felt like to live in a character - to allow yourself to get out of the way of a character.

I'm still with Kaufmann Forensic Actors, LLC eight years after that first gig - and I'm still learning every time I get the chance to live through the eyes of a child. The work Paul does with his company has made a measurable difference. Both the federal and state-level forensic agencies that work with Kaufmann Forensic Actors report that they've increased the effectiveness of prosecuting and convicting perpetrators who victimize children. Paul found a way to use theatre arts to do some good beyond entertainment and catharsis - he used it to make a difference, to truly better someone's life. What a gift.

―

We're driving toward the desert.

We're going to pull over pretty soon here. We all want to feel the sand under our feet. We've all smelled and stepped onto a sandy beach, but the desert promises to be different. Isn't it supposed to smell like sage in the desert...or something like that? I'm so excited. Something new. Something singular. This will be my first time. My first time in the desert. I hope it won't be my last. You always see the desert during the day in old western films, but we're going out there at night. Albuquerque has been an amazing trip. I've met so many friends of Paul on this trip. They've all been so kind - much like Paul himself. It's fun to celebrate good work. The work comes first, and then you get to play after.

Raise your face back toward the rush of air from the interstate. The air feels so fresh on your clean-shaven face. Wait, where's my attempt at a beard? Oh that's right, I shaved it to play a child this week. Moment of panic over. I had too much tonight. Ah hell, maybe you haven't had enough, boy.

Paul puts on the turn signal. "Let's pull over at this exit," he says. Everyone in the car concurs. I signify my approval with a private smile as I gaze at the huge moon that hovers overhead.

We're pulling off to the right, onto an exit ramp. We're driving toward something new. We're driving toward the desert.

———

There are many colors on the palette of Paul Kaufmann. Or perhaps he'd be the canvas. In any case, he's a well-travelled man with plenty of life's stories that he's willing to share. It might explain why he's heavily involved in an art form that exists through storytelling. Those who know him long

enough begin to gather a "greatest hits" from his storytelling repertoire - and if you happen to hear some of his stories more than once, it's a welcome repetition - it's never the same.
Many people have different relationships with Paul. He'll admit that there are some who have called him a pusher. In fact, a friend of his once gave him a t-shirt that read: "PUSHER."

And that word may mean various things to various people. But it means something specific to me. Something that's absolutely true about him.

I have only felt truly pushed by very few people. Paul is one of them. Paul believes in the intelligence of others. As a theatre artist he doesn't assume that audiences only want the safe and familiar. He doesn't take for granted the power of an audience's imagination or the possibility that they might become part of the creative process.

Paul wants a collective push for more from his fellow artists. Paul will look at the successes of an artistic expression, and then move quickly to an examination of the challenges, failures, and shortcomings of that same expression that was deemed a success. He's also not one to forgive ineffective or safe choices. Risk is necessary. Risk is the driving force of creation. We must strive for bold experiments. We must strive for new works. We must strive for high quality standards. We must forgive sparingly, while not allowing ourselves to forget. We must hold each other accountable. We must strive for more.

I can't tell you how many times I've had conversations with Paul that damn near infuriated me. A casual conversation about "what's been going on" and "what are you working on" can become a dialogue steeped in examination. These conversations often feature critical evaluations of the failings of local arts organizations, the reasons why certain people are respected or not, the standards of professional versus community theatre, and the local value of artists' talents and time. And many times I find myself screaming in my head, "What can I do about it? What can one person or two do about any of these issues?" Then I sleep on it, and wake up the next day realizing that I was the one letting the fire under my ass diminish. One person trying to make a difference is truly better than none, and why was I allowing myself to become complacent? After a while the lesson was learned, and now these conversations are welcome. You relearn to set an example rather than accept the circumstances.

Granted, I still find myself not tending the fire on occasion. However, a visit with Paul will open up the can of lighter fluid needed to arouse the flames back into their dance. So yes, Paul is a "pusher". He is pushing me to stay lit - to keep that fire burning and to keep striving for more.

We are no longer driving toward the desert. Alas, we are in the desert.

The car door is open, and my shoe finds compacted sand as I slide out of the seat. A few steps further and the sand loosens. The air is still and dry.

I look to one side and see some of my colleagues doing a jig or something. Why not dance in the desert? I join in. As I sway side to side I see the glow of a casino in the distance. In the other direction, an ocean of stars overhead and an infinity of sand that grows dimmer and dimmer the further it stretches beyond the moonlight. This is all new wonderful.

What's out there? I have no idea, but I'm sure it'd be new, too. But don't go wandering away from the group, boy. You've seen way too many movies with some person lost in the desert seeing mirages of some beautiful woman and not having a drop of water to drink, and that would not be preferred on the sober side of daylight. I stare ahead letting my imagination create what I can't see in the dark. A cactus? Yes, a cactus and a tumbleweed resting between trips. A jackrabbit, too. But no snakes. This is a snakeless desert, right? Ah, the comfort of denial.

After a spell, Paul's voice cuts through my self-imposed mirage with, "Did we all love the desert?" Resounding affirmations from all. "Well, we should probably head back to the city." He's right. We have to fly back east early in the morning.

We beat our shoes on the side of the car releasing a rainstorm of sand beneath our feet before we re-enter the rental. This trip has been amazing. Something new. Something different.

There's a stereotype in existence that paints artists as externally tormented or self-tormenting creators. I prefer the notion that artistic expression is a joyous happening. It's a moment to connect with other artists or the people who experience your art. It's a moment to share and learn. What could be more joyous than that?

One of the joys of creating is being able to tap into that younger-self we keep buried under our finances, our relationship stresses, our egos, our struggles with health, and our misunderstandings of each other and our hopes for the world around us. Paul has taught me to celebrate that aspect of artistry. Children, if left to their own devices, would possibly stay in a hypnotic state of play and pretend: conversing with imaginary friends, imagining a tree fort is a pirate ship carrying treasure, pretending that wearing your dad's straw Masters hat makes you Indiana Jones. We become adults and it becomes hard to succumb to our imagination. But Paul would say as artists, we still can. We can imagine and we can work toward making it a reality. We can play, and we should play often.

I've only scratched the surface when it comes to the many ways Paul Kaufmann has influenced me, and I can only hope that other artists have a Paul in their lives. He's taught me so much about friendship, travel, acting, storytelling, and myself. He has so much passion for creation that often times you can find him rehearsing a show, and then learn he's also working on a few original scripts, a new visual art piece, and getting his designs turned into wallpaper or fabric. He's letting himself play.

As I look to the future of my artistic endeavors I keep Paul's voice in the back of my head. We must continue to create something new. We must examine ourselves and each other to assess our shortcomings. We must receive the knowledge of those shortcomings as a gift and be proactive about improving them. We must strive for more from ourselves and others. We must be pushers.

We must welcome the unknown. We must welcome firsts. So let's set our sails to the west.

We're driving toward the desert.

About the Authors

JENNIFER BARTELL

Jennifer Bartell has an MFA from the University of South Carolina. Her poetry has appeared in *Callaloo, pluck!: The Journal of Affrilachian Arts & Culture, the museum of americana, decomP, Composite {Arts Magazine}*, and others. She is also a Callaloo Fellow.

CYNTHIA BOITER

Cynthia Boiter is the editor of several collections and anthologies about South Carolina authors and artists, as well as the editor-in-chief of *Jasper Magazine* and the author of *Buttered Biscuits: Short Stories about the South.* She is the recipient of the 2014 Elizabeth O'Neill Verner Governor's Award for the Arts.

DEBRA DANIEL

Debra A. Daniel (novel *Woman Commits Suicide in Dishwasher* & poetry chapbooks, *The Downward Turn of August & As Is*) was twice named SC Arts Commission Poetry Fellow and won the Guy Owen Prize. Work has appeared in: *The Los Angeles Review, Smokelong, Pequin, Inkwell, Southern Poetry Review, Tar River.*

CLAIR DELUNE

Clair DeLune has hosted an educational roots music radio program, Blues Moon Radio, on WUSC-FM each Tuesday evening, since 1990. She is a musician and fan, author, editor, photographer, professor, counselor, radio host, media producer and historian. She appreciates her good fortune to have become so close with Drink Small, and feels truly honored to be able to share his stories and philosophy with others. DeLune is deeply grateful to Muddy Ford Press for asking her to contribute to this book.

JANE GARI

S. Jane Gari lives in Elgin, South Carolina with her husband and daughter. Her memoir, *Losing the Dollhouse* was released in February 2015 by Touch Point Press. You can learn more about her writing and message at www.sjanegari.com.

WILLIAM GARLAND

William Garland teaches English and Creative Writing at Montverde Academy in Montverde, FL. He is a graduate of MFA program in creative writing from the University of South Carolina. His work appears in *HOOT, The Dr. T.J. Eckleburg Review, Revolution House, The Dead Mule School of Southern Literature, Real South Magazine, Jasper Magazine* and other literary journals and anthologies.

KARA GUNTER

Kara Gunter is a professional visual artist who teaches art at the University of South Carolina and is the visual arts editor for *Jasper Magazine*.

KRISTINE HARTVIGSEN

Kristine Hartvigsen is a contributor and past associate editor of *Jasper Magazine*, a former editor of *South Carolina Business, Lake Murray-Columbia,* and *Columbia Northeast* magazines. She is the author of the chapbook, *To the Wren Nesting*, published by Muddy Ford Press in 2012.

RACHEL HAYNIE

Rachel Haynie writes frequently about art – for *Jasper, Columbia Living Magazine and Blue Fish Digest* – and history. The City of Columbia and Richland One selected the USC graduate's youth biography *First, You Explore: The Story of the Young Charles Townes,* from USC Press, for Together We Can Read 2015. For more mature readers *Charles H. Townes and a Beam Straight to the Stars* has just been released.

CHAD HENDERSON

Chad Henderson is the Artistic Director of Trustus Theatre, a professional theatre in Columbia, SC. He has directed many productions at various theatres in South Carolina including Trustus Theatre, Workshop Theatre of South Carolina, The Columbia Children's Theatre, Theatre South Carolina, Spartanburg Next Stage, and the Spartanburg Youth Theatre. Henderson has also completed two residencies at The Studios of Key West in Florida.

AUGUST KRICKEL

August Krickel writes about theatre in Columbia, SC and is the former theatre editor for *Jasper Magazine*.

SUSAN LENZ

Susan Lenz is an internationally renowned fiber and installation artist who is based in Columbia, SC and has traveled to multiple juried art residencies throughout the world. She was voted Jasper Visual Artist of the Year in 2012.

JAMES D. MCCALLISTER

James D. McCallister, a lifelong resident of the South Carolina midlands, is the author of two novels, *King's Highway* (Red Letter Press, 2007) and *Fellow Traveler* (Muddy Ford Press, 2012), as well as a variety of creative nonfiction publications. A two-time SC Fiction Project honoree as well as a Faulkner-Wisdom Competition and *Saturday Evening Post* short story finalist, McCallister adjuncts in creative writing at Midlands Technical College.

LAURIE BROWNELL MCINTOSH

Visual artist Laurie McIntosh's work has shown throughout South Carolina and in Florida. She is the author *of All the In Between: My Story of Agnes,* published by Muddy Ford Press in 2012.

MICHAEL MILLER

Columbia based writer Michael Miller is the author of the short story collection *Lonesome Pines*, published in 2008, as well as a biography of the rock band Hootie and the Blowfish, published in 1997.

KYLE PETERSEN

Kyle Petersen is a doctoral candidate in English at the University of South Carolina who writes about music and occasionally film for a number of publications throughout the Southeast. He is the assistant editor of *Jasper Magazine*.

BRANDI PERRY

Brandi L. Perry is a James Dickey Fellow and inaugural SPARC Fellowship awardee as well as the editor of *The Art of Medicine in Metaphors: A Collection of Poems and Narratives* (2013).

TOM POLAND

Tom Poland writes about the South, its people, land, and culture. He covers back roads, forgotten places, and vestiges of bygone times. Much of it ends up in books. A Georgian and University of Georgia alumnus, he lives in Columbia where he writes about Georgialina, his native land.

RANDY SPENCER

Randy Spencer is a physician and poet living in Chapin, South Carolina who recieved his MFA in Poetry from the University of South Carolina in 2002. He has published two chapbooks of poetry, *The Failure of Magic* and, most recently, *What the Body Knows*, published through the South Carolina Poetry Initiative in 2010.

JON TUTTLE

Jon Tuttle is Professor of English and Director of University Honors at Francis Marion University. His published plays include *A Fish Story, Terminal Café, The Hammerstone, Drift, The White Problem, Holy Ghost, The Sweet Abyss*, and *The Palace of the Moorish Kings*. He has received fellowships from the South Carolina Arts Commission and the South Carolina Academy of Authors, on whose Board of Governors he now serves.

SUSAN LEVI WALLACH

Susan Levi Wallach was the recipient of the 2014 Thomas Wolfe Fiction Prize. Recently, her work has appeared in the *Southern California Review, American Athenaeum*, and *The Moth*. She has an MFA from Vermont College of Fine Arts and is a freelance copyeditor.

About the Cover Artist

MATT CATOE

Matt Catoe was born in Lexington, South Carolina in 1987. He works predominantly in drawing and painting mediums. Matt completed his undergraduate studies in 2012, with a BA in Media Arts and a BFA in Studio Art with a focus in drawing. Following his graduation, Matt spent a semester in Budapest, Hungary studying at the Hungarian University of Fine Arts. Matt has been included in group shows in Columbia and Budapest, as well as traveling exhibitions at the University of South Carolina, MICA, the Kansas City Art Institute, and the Minneapolis College of Art and Design.

Matt currently lives in Columbia and works as the Program Manager at Tapp's Arts Center.

www.ingramcontent.com/pod-product-compliance
Lightning Source LLC
Chambersburg PA
CBHW071622080526
44588CB00010B/1235